DERMOCRACY

Dr SHARAD P. PAUL practises and teaches internationally in the field of cutaneous oncology and is involved in developing innovative skincare products and cosmetics. In 2003, he received a Health Innovation Award. In 2008, he was featured in international editions of *Time* magazine in an article titled 'Open Heart Surgeon', and was called 'Renaissance Man' by *New Zealand Herald*'s *Canvas* magazine and 'polymath' by *Good* magazine. Paul writes literary fiction and runs literacy programmes for disadvantaged children via his Baci Foundation charitable trust. In 2012, he was awarded the New Zealand Medical Association's highest honour, the Chair's Award, and was a finalist for the New Zealander of the Year Award.

His first novel, *Cool Cut* (Picador, 2007), was reissued as an extended edition by HarperCollins as *The Kite Flyers* in 2013. Paul's second novel, *To Kill a Snow Dragonfly*, was published by Fourth Estate in 2012. *Skin: A Biography* (Fourth Estate, 2012), his first creative non-fiction work, was an ambitious mapping of the history and science of skin and skin colour.

DERMOCRACY

For Brown Skin, by Brown Skin

THE DEFINITIVE ASIAN SKINCARE GUIDE

SHARAD P. PAUL

Collins

First published in India in 2014 by Collins
An Imprint of HarperCollins *Publishers*

Copyright © Sharad P. Paul 2014

P-ISBN: 978-93-5136-341-5
E-ISBN: 978-93-5136-342-2

2 4 6 8 10 9 7 5 3 1

HarperCollins *Publishers*
A-75, Sector 57, Noida, Uttar Pradesh 201301, India
77-85 Fulham Palace Road, London W6 8JB, United Kingdom
Hazelton Lanes, 55 Avenue Road, Suite 2900, Toronto, Ontario M5R 3L2
and 1995 Markham Road, Scarborough, Ontario M1B 5M8, Canada
25 Ryde Road, Pymble, Sydney, NSW 2073, Australia
10 East 53rd Street, New York NY 10022, USA

Typeset in 10/14 Melior LT Std
Jojy Philip New Delhi 110 015

Printed and bound at
Thomson Press (India) Ltd

This book is for India and Indians everywhere;
I may live outside India, but India lives
in my brown skin

Contents

Foreword

As I travelled through India for book launches in 2007, I was astounded by how much of the skincare information in magazines was generally borrowed from Western publications. There was very little information on – or indeed awareness of – the brown and Asian skin types and their special considerations.

My original residency training was in plastic surgery. In my work as a skin cancer specialist, skincare researcher, lecturer at universities and as developer of Mikanis, the first skincare range designed specifically for brown skin, I have come to realize that each skin type has unique characteristics. One kind of treatment does not fit all.

This book isn't about the skincare range I've created for brown skin or selling products. This is about my passion for educating people about care for brown skin.

The multi-billion dollar skincare industry sells most of its products on emotion, not science. When I first developed products for brown skin, it was because I was looking for skincare solutions for myself or my family. Most products did not suit the type of brown skin I have. I prescribe for my clients and patients the same treatments that I would for myself or my family. There is no animal testing for any products I make – other than on myself.

The twenty-four skincare tips in this book are based on common questions that patients, friends, aestheticians and beauty salon owners have asked me over the years. This is not a medical book and it does not deal with prescription medication or drugs. I have written this for beauty salon therapists, aestheticians and for everybody interested in the care of brown skin. The focus of this book is to give you advice on understanding the unique qualities and issues of brown skin, and managing it better – thereby making you look your best. I have also given you some home-made recipes to try out. Any medical or anatomical terms I use in the first chapter are explained in simple terms. Also, while I do mention some attributes of Caucasian or white skin, that is not the focus here, because this is the skincare book for brown, and indeed Asian, skin.

I hope you will find *Dermocracy* a useful resource and reference guide, and that it will answer all questions you have about dealing with the brown skin type. Be proud of your skin; I am.

Dr SHARAD P. PAUL
MD, MPhil.

Dedication

I would like to dedicate this book to my late uncle Dr A.S. Thambiah. Uncle Bobby, as I knew him, established the Department of Dermatology at Madras Medical College and Government General Hospital. The dermatology department, the oldest clinical sub-speciality, was founded by Lt Col J.M. Skinner of the Indian Medical Services. As my uncle was a decorated officer in the Indian Army, he succeeded Lt Col Skinner. In 1961, the first professorial chair was instituted, and Dr A.S. Thambiah was made the first professor. He quickly developed an international reputation as one of India's foremost dermatologists. He modelled the department after the Institute of Dermatology at St John's Hospital, London, and to his clinical dermatology division he added a dermatopathology service, a mycology wing and a contact dermatitis clinic.

Uncle Bobby lived his life for dermatology. He practised until the very end and was interested in my career in plastic surgery, especially my interest in cutaneous surgery.

He had no TV or a wife, but he needed neither; his time was filled with solving skin problems of several million grateful patients, and the rest was spent in conversations with God. I remember the legendary queues outside his house at 5.30 a.m.

when the first patients would try to get in. While he charged
no fees from students, widows, policemen or servicemen, he
treated young and old, the wealthy and the poor alike. When
Madras University celebrated its centenary, he was the only
professor to be awarded the DSc. as an honour. He did not live
to see this book completed. Fare thee well, Uncle Bobby. May
you rest in peace.

1

Oily v. Dry Skin

I have heard that skin is divided into oily and dry skin types. Where does brown skin fit in? My main complaint is that my nose gets shiny and I have to keep dabbing talcum powder on it.

...

In most people, skin type is a combination of dry and oily skin, although some people have excessively dry or oily skin.

Brown skin is usually what we call 'combination oily' skin. The increased sebaceous activity and oiliness are concentrated around the central forehead, nose and skin of upper lip/chin – in other words, in the T-zone. This is why people in the Indian subcontinent tend to powder their shiny noses.

'T-zone' (see Figure 1) is the term used to denote the central forehead (with extensions to either side like in a T) and a straight downward limb that

Figure 1: The T-zone

includes the nose, upper lip and chin. This area is more prone to sebaceous activity and is therefore predisposed to acne and an oily sheen.

The T-zone tends to have larger hair follicles because the oil secreted by sebaceous (oil) glands uses the follicle openings to exit the skin surface. This increased oil production leads to widened pores. The result? Skin that could appear shiny and pores that could get clogged, leading to open comedones or blackheads (see Figure 2). If this comedo remains closed, it is prone to inflammation and infection due to trapped debris, which results in the formation of whiteheads. Blackheads, being open, are less likely to get infected or inflamed.

In people prone to blackheads or whiteheads, it is important to exfoliate skin. We will discuss this later.

However, as you move on to the cheeks, the pores are smaller and the skin is more likely to become dry in winter. If you do not moisturize this area, the skin there could begin to peel. This is especially important at night and in winter.

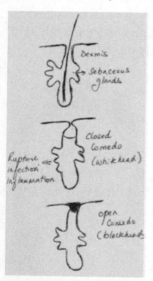

Figure 2: Formation of acne, blackheads and whiteheads

Perhaps one of the easiest ways to tell what type of skin someone has is to simply observe the size of the pores. The pores are more noticeable on the nose and immediately surrounding areas, and not as much on the cheeks. Sometimes, on the nose, what you see will be clogged pores. The larger the pores on the nose, the more oily your skin will be.

It is an interesting fact that rather than having either completely dry or oily skin, most Indians have central areas of oiliness and peripheral facial areas that are prone to dehydration and dryness.

You may ask why bother with this characterization of skin type? In my view, skincare regimens need to be tailored for different skin types. There are no absolute rules, but an understanding of specific properties of a certain skin colour helps. Some skin types are prone to dryness, as in very fair redheads. Skin prone to dryness is more susceptible to skin diseases like eczema and dermatitis. In other white-skinned people, the skin may be a combination, but is usually what we call 'combination dry' – this means that the pores are visible just in the middle of the nose and the rest of the face is dry. Brown skin is 'combination oily' in which case the pores are visible on the nose and the immediately surrounding cheeks and chin. Because of this, most brown skin is suited to light, rather than heavy emollients, moisturizers or oily moisturizers like cocoa or shea butter.

When I design day creams for brown skin, I often specifically use a light silicone-based moisturizer, which reduces shininess or oiliness of skin. I have developed my own natural biotechnological cocktail using various plant-based compounds to reduce ageing, damage due to ultra violet (UV) radiation and pigmentation. A lot of people use whitening

> **Recipe for home-made moisturizer**
>
> Rose water with a few drops of almond oil (number of drops depends on how oily or dry the skin is) with finely ground beeswax stirred in (needs to be melted and cooled; I use a small metal bowl floating in a large pan of hot water to melt the beeswax). Remember that almond oil, like many vegetable oils, is comedogenic (by which I mean that it could lead to blackheads or whiteheads) and can lead to pimples, so I'd add only one or two drops.

creams, but there is really no 'healthy' way to whiten skin and as such bleaches can be harmful.

On a fundamental level, modern lifestyles dry skin out and moisturizing is the best thing you can do for it. Like I said earlier, light moisturizers are better for brown and Asian skin.

Key points

- Brown skin is what we call 'combination oily' skin.

- Brown skin is not suited to heavy moisturizers – these will make skin sweat.

- I do not recommend using moisturizers like cocoa or shea butter for the face in case of brown skin.

- Home-made light moisturizer ingredients: rose water with a few drops of almond oil and mixed with finely ground melted and cooled beeswax.

2

Gel v. Foam

I feel there is a difference when I use a foaming cleanser rather than a shave gel. Is this simply my imagination? On a related note, how does one choose a cleanser, and is it better to get one that foams?

...

I'm impressed with your observation. You are quite right in noticing differences between foams and gels. It is true that foaming shaving creams and shaving gels have different properties and cleansing abilities even if they are not obvious to everyone. It is important to understand not just what makes cleansers foam, but also the attributes of brown skin, which, as I have already said, is usually 'combination oily' skin.

Important factors in this discussion are:

1. How much surfactant does the cleanser contain? What makes cleansers foam? It is the presence of ingredients called surfactants that determines the foaming abilities of a cleanser. Surfactants in effect reduce surface tension in a liquid and make it 'glide' across skin. The more surfactant a cleanser contains, the more it will foam.
2. The more oily the skin, the more foamy the cleanser needs to be. This is because surfactants are like

detergents and are needed to remove excess oils from the skin. So if your skin is very oily, you not only need a foaming facial cleanser, but also a shaving product that foams a lot – essentially, you need more surfactant to cleanse properly. This will give you a nice and close shave. And the more surfactant the cleanser has, the more foam it will produce. Surfactants are commonly sulphates or sulphonates and usually listed at the top of the ingredient list in cleansers (meaning they make up higher concentrations of the product). I generally make sure I avoid sulphates in my products. Acne skin cleansers are generally foaming as acne-prone skin tends to be oily. However, these acne cleansers contain surfactants to which an antibacterial like salicylic acid or benzoyl peroxide is added. (In the acne cleansers I make, I use salicylic acid, because I have noted more skin peeling with benzoyl peroxide in brown skin. However, both are useful and both can cause some peeling if overused.)

3. But what happens if someone has dry skin? Dry skin is the result of a damaged oil layer. Here, adding a surfactant will not help, because we need oil to repair the oil layer first. So most cleansers for dry skin contain oils or emollients and these are often called cleansing milks or look more like a moisturizing cream. I don't normally recommend these on brown skin, unless someone is prone to dermatitis or eczema.

4. The question of cleansers is one that concerns men and women alike. Removing make-up is a different issue altogether. Because make-up can clog pores and adhere to skin, and a foaming cleanser with surfactant may not remove it effectively. So one needs to use an oily non-foaming cleanser or cleansing milk to remove make-up, especially if one is heavily made-up. Or simply make a

cold cream cleanser yourself. I have listed a cold cream recipe later in this book.

5.   One method to manage combination oily skin if you are using make-up is this: use a foaming cleanser during the morning to wash your face and then use day cream. At night, use a cleansing milk to remove the make-up and just wipe your face with the cold cream.

Recipe for home-made cleanser

One tablespoon of pure honey, one tablespoon of lemon juice (contains Vitamin C), half a cup of spring or distilled water, one tablespoon of brown sugar (helps cleanse pores), one tablespoon of vegetable glycerine (use two tablespoons if you have dry skin; vegetable glycerine is also sometimes called glycerine or vegetable glycerol. It is a sugar usually derived from plant oils. Vegetable glycerine is used to make sweeteners and used in cosmetics as well. It is also used instead of alcohol to extract botanicals for use in cosmetics and medicines. It is easily available in pharmacies). Mix these together and you have a good home-made cleanser. To remove heavy make-up, you'll need to add more glycerine as you would for dry skin. This one works well once you've learnt to titrate (or measure and adjust) the glycerine content up or down to suit your skin's level of oiliness

Key points

- Cleansers can be foaming or non-foaming.
- The more foaming a cleanser, the more surfactant it contains.
- Avoid sulphonates; sulphates are OK.
- The more oily your skin, the more foaming the cleanser needs to be.
- If your skin is very dry, or if you are removing heavy make-up, you need a cleansing milk or cream that does not foam.
- For men, while choosing a shaving cream, go for a foaming cream if your skin is combination skin. If you are prone to dry skin, go for a shaving gel that does not foam much.
- Home-made cleanser ingredients: honey/lemon juice/glycerine/brown sugar.

3

Shampoo v. Conditioner

I've heard you say that brown haircare regimens must be 'ulta' or the opposite of what you'd normally expect. So when I use a shampoo, must I always use conditioner afterwards?
...

While brown skin is combination oily, black or brown hair is more prone to oiliness. This is no accident, but an adaptation to climate. Tropical climates are notorious for their heat and dust. Of course, in modern cities everywhere, pollution is also becoming a major factor, but this is a recent phenomenon in the larger scheme of things.

The oil layer of the scalp essentially performs two functions:

1. It stops dust and irritants from damaging the scalp.
2. It forms a lipid barrier, which prevents loss of water due to heat and sweat.

This may seem paradoxical, but this lipid or fat layer in the skin is most important – if one has a deficient or damaged lipid layer, one is more prone to scalp diseases.

When I first began researching brown skin in particular, I was not attempting to reinvent the wheel, so to speak. I was attempting to look at ancient remedies (also marvel at) and understand the science behind ancient advice and relate that with modern lifestyles. Most of the times when I develop skincare products I research both ancient Ayurvedic remedies as well as traditional advice that have been passed down by our grandmothers. There always seems to be sound scientific basis for practices that have been adopted over generations.

The 'oil bath' is a well-established Indian ritual. As a child growing up in India, I remember that many elders and grandparents advocated oil baths – they would apply oil to their skin and then have a bath an hour or so later. Another widely used method was massaging the scalp with oil before a bath. When I was a toddler, the domestic help at home used to apply coconut oil to my hair before brushing it. In the southern part of India, coconut oil is the norm and in the north, almond oil is also used.

Traditionally, in India, both coconut and mustard oil were used as massage oils before bathing. Which is better? In Ayurveda, mustard oil was considered a 'hot' oil and therefore used in the winter months; coconut oil was considered a 'cool' oil and used in the summer months. In south India, where it is always summery, coconut is the primary oil. This classification has nothing to do with actual body temperature. In Ayurveda, foods can also be hot or cold. For example, foods like chicken, garlic and cloves are considered 'hot'. Mustard oil, however, can cause skin inflammation and there have been several reports in medical journals of rashes occurring after using mustard oil. Therefore, of the two, coconut oil is the lesser irritant.

There is another difference between the two oils. When it comes to coconut oil, the same oil is used for cooking and on skin. However, mustard oil comes in two variants – the one used for cooking is made by pressing the seeds; the essential oil used on skin is made by grinding the seeds, mixing with water and distilling the mixture.

Oil baths served an important function. It is an established medical fact that using soaps, or washing too often, damages the vital oil layer of the skin and scalp. It is clear that ancient Indians were well aware of this. Their use of oil on the skin and scalp before applying soap (or its equivalent) prevented the oil layer from being stripped away. The oil thus checked skin dehydration.

I doubt our modern lifestyles would allow people to walk around with oily hair any longer. Further, using oil on the hair can lead to forehead pimples, as I'll explain later. This is where the 'ulta' or 'opposite' method of hair washing is handy, especially for those with dark hair.

Indian hair is different because it is mostly wavy or curly and not dead-straight like those of other Asians, say the Chinese or Koreans. It is also thicker than the hair of Caucasians and similar to that of Latin Americans. The more curly the hair, the more curved the hair follicle (I'll come to that in a bit). Most shampoos contain sulphates, which can actually worsen the frizziness of dark hair. Using a conditioner first (in earlier times, people simply used a diluted version of baking soda) ensures that your hair retains the moisture and therefore its suppleness and elasticity.

> **Recipe for home-made conditioner**
>
> You can, if you wish, make a home-made conditioner of diluted baking soda using one teaspoon for half a cup of water and mix with an equal portion of coconut oil.

Sodium lauryl sulphate (SLS) and sodium laureth sulphate (SLES) are chemicals often found in shampoos and cleansers. It is best to avoid them as they can be irritants, allergens and also toxic. In general sulphates are bad; sulphonates are good in cleansers.

However, as we discussed earlier, Asian and Latin American conditions are full of dust and pollution, both of which cause residues that weigh the hair down and also lead to hair losing its bounce. Applying shampoo after using a conditioner removes these residues without damaging hair. So for dark hair, when you are in tropical conditions, I would definitely recommend using a conditioner before shampooing. I travel a lot and find that my hair behaves differently while in India and in Australasia. When in tropical conditions, using a conditioner before shampooing definitely helps.

Key points

- Dark hair is prone to oiliness.
- Darker the skin, the more curvy the hair follicle.
- Using a conditioner first retains moisture in brown skin and keeps it supple, especially in tropical conditions.
- Following a conditioner, use a gentle shampoo to remove residues and dust from hair.
- Home-made hair conditioner: mix baking soda and water with coconut oil.

4

SPF 15 v. SPF 50

Can you explain sun protection and SPF? When I use a sunblock with an SPF rating of 30 or higher, it makes me sweat. Also, I see some cricketers looking like they have put white paint on their cheek – is this really necessary, or are they simply copying Australian cricketers? ...

We needed a cricket question in here; it is a book for Indians after all!

This question is aligned to my main research interest outside wound healing and developing cosmetics, because my major work is as a skin cancer surgeon and lecturer. Simply put, SPF stands for 'sun protection factor'. So in theory, an SPF of 10 provides ten times the sun protection, i.e., you can stay in the sun ten times longer than the time your skin would normally be able to tolerate it. However, for Indian and brown skin types we need to re-evaluate the significance of SPF. Brown skin does not get as damaged as white skin in the sun, nor is it as prone to skin cancer. But, of course, our brown skin does develop pigmentation and other effects of solar damage.

Australasia, i.e., Australia and New Zealand (also including the neighbouring Pacific islands, where I spend most of my time, has the highest UV indices in the world. But because most of the population that migrated there was of Celtic descent, i.e., belonging to Scotland/Ireland/northern England, their skin was most unsuited to the sun in these parts of the southern hemisphere. These people also brought their lifestyles with them – a fondness for lying on the beach, recreational fishing, sailing and the like. These factors not only cause severe sun damage, which leads to skin cancer in Australasia, but also make white skin turn leathery because of sun damage. A colleague of mine, who is a neurologist, used to inject Botox (Botox was used to treat facial tics before it became fashionable for cosmetic procedures) on patients in the UK. He has moved to Australia now and does the same to patients there. He swears that in Australia the skin is a lot tougher than in the UK to penetrate with a needle. As most of my skin cancer patients are of Celtic origin, I tell them that it is essentially a problem with migration – a particular skin type migrated to the wrong location for that type. Of course, evolution is at work and in 2,000 years, if human beings are still around, we shall see thicker, browner and more adapted skin in this same group of people.

Let me take a moment to explain that better. The manner in which melanin, or the brown pigment, is located in brown skin protects the cells from DNA damage caused by the sun. Therefore, brown skin type has a very low risk of skin cancer when compared to white skin types. To give meaningful advice on SPF, one needs to understand the UV index. The UV index is a mathematical model that was developed by researchers to provide a uniform method of recording UV radiation from the sun. Until such a standardization was available, the difference in latitudes and hemispheres meant that it was difficult to accurately assess the damage caused by the sun's rays.

The UV index is a computerized model that calculates ozone levels and relates it to UV incidence, thus putting a number to the incoming UV radiation level on the ground. This takes into account cloud cover (by factoring in a cloud modifying factor or CMF) and also the elevation of the place.

Weather reports speak of the UV index measure to help people protect their skin. When the UV index was first developed, nobody realized that the highest UV levels due to location and ozone depletion would be close to the South Pole. Carnarvon in western Australia has recorded a UV index of 17 and a UV index of 12 is often seen in New Zealand in peak summer time. The UV index registers maximal readings between hours of noon to 3 p.m., so it is generally best not to step out in the sun during those hours (if possible, avoid going out from 11 a.m. to 4 p.m.). In the Indian skin type, exposure during those hours will lead to maximum tanning and darker pigmentation of skin. The UV index in New Delhi in summer is around 10.

How does knowing the UV index help us plan our sun exposure?

Skin type 1 Maximum time in the sun = 67 minutes/ UV index	Skin type 2 Maximum time in the sun = 100 minutes/UV index
Skin type 3 Maximum time in the sun = 200 minutes/UV index	Skin type 4 Maximum time in the sun = 300 minutes/UV index

Figure 3: The UV Index

The UV index uses what are called the Fitzpatrick skin types. Type 1 skin is redhead–green eyes (like Irish skin); type 2 is blonde–blue eyes; type 3 skin is white skin–dark hair (like Italian skin), types 4 and 5 predominantly make up Indian and Latino skin types (type 4 is 'fair' Indian/Latino skin and type 5 is 'dark' Indian skin); type 6 is really black skin like African skin type or in some parts of south India or Sri Lanka. Types 5 and 6 don't get any significant sun damage.

As Figure 3 illustrates, type 4 skin can have safe sun exposure of 300 minutes/UV index. As the UV index of New Delhi is typically 10 in summer, safe sun exposure time (without tanning) would only be thirty minutes. If one used a sunblock of SPF 15, one could expose oneself for fifteen times the safe limit, provided the sunblock was reapplied every few hours. Many ingredients in sunblocks can stimulate tanning in brown skin types (because sunblocks can contain UV absorbers that generate heat), and many are using a sunscreen to reduce this tanning effect, which is a defence mechanism. I only recommend a low SPF rating for brown skin – generally SPF 15 is enough. Even with a sunblock on, I do not advocate exposure between hours of noon to 3 p.m. unless it is needed for occupational purposes. Peak sun exposure causes more photo damage, which is related to pigmentation or ageing problems. For sportsmen, especially cricketers who have to stay out all day in the sun, I would recommend that they use a sunblock with an SPF rating of 15 to 30 and reapply during lunch and tea breaks. I have developed sunblocks with an SPF 15 rating, and they do not feel oily as they have been specially engineered for the combination oily skin in Asia and Latin America.

UV radiation is divided into the following types:

- UVC: 100–280 nm
- UVB: 280–320 nm
- UVA: 320–400 nm

While about 97 per cent of UV rays from the sun are filtered out by the atmosphere, the 3 per cent that reaches the earth's surface is made up of both UVA and UVB radiation. In general, UVA radiation can penetrate through transparent clothing or glass, and most sunscreen lotions (except those with specific UVA screens) do not protect against UVA radiation. UVA rays have been implicated in causing melanomas, the deadliest form of skin cancer.

UVB radiation generally causes sunburns in fair skin and tanning in brown skin types. It may sometimes cause peeling of skin. Peeling is also a sign of skin damage, occurring when the body kills its own cells in an attempt to repair the damage to the outer layer.

How does UV damage lead to skin cancer and pigmentation?

When the skin is exposed to UV radiation, the photons cause damage to the DNA by altering the nucleic acid sequences into 'dimers', i.e., abnormal sequences. If these sequences are not repaired, the abnormal DNA divides abnormally, leading to production of skin cancer cells later on. Therefore, the body mobilizes certain enzymes to repair it. In brown skin, we are blessed with an abundance of melanin: this means that the large melanosome shields the nucleus where the DNA is stored, and the bodily enzymes are more than enough to repair the damage the UV radiation causes. In red-headed or Celtic white-skinned people, those lacking these melanosomes to shield the nucleus, the DNA sustains severe damage. The enzymes stores may not always be enough to properly repair the damage, leading to a higher risk of skin cancer later on in life.

I often use diabetes as an analogy when teaching my students. Everyone is born with a supply of insulin in the pancreas. Of course, some people are born with a genetic deficiency and this leads to Type-1 diabetes in childhood; this is the rarer form and these people need insulin injections throughout their lives. Most people, however, develop Type-2 diabetes because they have eaten too much over time, and this 'pigging out' makes them run out of insulin stores in middle age. Therefore, they need to take tablets that can increase insulin production or improve tissue uptake; some of these people end up on insulin injections. Type-2 diabetes is becoming all too common in India (with our fondness for sweets and overeating) these days.

This is a good analogy to understand UV damage. Some people are born with a deficiency of the enzymes that repair this DNA damage from UV radiation. This genetic deficiency is found in a condition called *xeroderma pigmentosum*. These people develop a multitude of skin cancers. However, in white-skinned people who have had a lot of sun exposure or have used tanning beds, the skin gets damaged until bodily systems can no longer cope – leading to skin cancer. Fortunately for brown skin, the large melanosome sits above the nucleus and shields it from sun damage and therefore we don't develop skin cancers (and hence don't develop 'Type-2' sun damage). This stimulation of melanin is, therefore, a defence mechanism. Which is why brown skin has a propensity to tan or become darker when exposed to the sun.

Having extolled the virtues of melanin, I must say that the presence of these large pigment cells leads to problems relating to pigmentation, i.e., dark patches, which, while not dangerous, can be a cosmetic nuisance.

Many dermatologists recommend SPF 30 for all skin types. However, given that all sunblocks contain sunscreens that can be absorbed by the skin, the long-term effects of such chemicals are unknown. Also, sunblocks were originally developed as suntan lotions; many sunblocks stimulate tanning in brown skin (this happens due to the UV-absorbing properties of sunscreens, which generate heat).

I recommend a sunblock of SPF 15 to 30 for Indian skin types. You may have to reapply at midday, so that it lasts all day in hot sun conditions. If you use a very high-SPF sunscreen it may look like you have applied face paint (as some higher-SPF 30–70 sunblocks tend to do) or make your face look oily.

Cricketers or sportspeople who are likely to stay out in the sun all day will find that sweat could wash the sunscreen away. It is important that they reapply sunscreen during lunch breaks, etc.

There's an interesting bit of myth busting I'd like to do here. Unlike popular perception, an SPF of 30 in your sunscreen filters out only 4 per cent more UV when compared to an SPF of 15, i.e., 97 per cent versus 93 per cent. The higher you increase the SPF, the smaller the increase. An SPF of 50 only filters out 98 per cent of UV rays. Essentially, higher SPF levels do not mean an incrementally higher UV filtering effect. In fact, the US Food and Drug Administration's recent guidelines prohibit sunscreens or cosmetics from claiming an SPF >50 as it gives users a false sense of security. However, in stores I still see sunscreens that claim higher SPF values.

I tell my students that the easy way to remember this is that SPF 15 lets in one in fifteen harmful sunrays, while SPF 30 lets in one in thirty, and SPF 50 one in fifty.

Let's not forget that melanin is a sunscreen. A sunscreen with an SPF of 2 would allow you to double your sun exposure. If we study the sun protection factor of melanin, we will note that melanin (and brown skin has plenty of it) has an inherent SPF of 2 to 4. In other words, it will let in one in two to one in four burning rays, and therefore absorb between 25 to 75 per cent of UV rays, usually around 50 per cent in brown skin.

Key points

- Indian and Asian skin generally belong to Fitzpatrick skin types 4 to 6.
- Avoid the sun between 12 noon and 3 p.m.
- Use a sunblock, but SPF 15–30 is enough.
- Look up the UV index for the day and plan accordingly.
- If playing sport out in the open all day, it is important to reapply sunscreen during breaks.

5

Exfoliating v. Peeling

I just went to a beauty salon and the therapist suggested that I use an exfoliator. What is an exfoliator and how does it help my skin? Is there any difference between an exfoliator and a peel?

...

Skin exfoliation has been practised since ancient times. Exfoliation is essentially scrubbing skin to remove the outermost layer of dead cells. A peel causes skin to, well, peel – the theory being that the new layer is more evenly pigmented or textured. Simply put, a peel goes deeper than exfoliation. Technically, we could say all peels exfoliate, but not all exfoliators will peel the skin. When we discuss skin anatomy in detail later on, we'll see that the outermost layer, i.e., the epidermis, is essentially composed of 'dead' cells or cells that have no direct blood supply. Blood supply to the skin is located deeper in the dermis. In ancient times, people scrubbed their skin with coarse sea salt to exfoliate. Even now, sea salt makes for a good home-made exfoliator. Another home-made exfoliator that was used in some hill stations in India was coarsely ground coffee beans. It is rumoured that wives of maharajas used crushed diamonds as exfoliators, and some expensive skin exfoliators have recently been promoting the use of crushed diamonds. My philosophy is to use renewable sources in nature whenever feasible, and while crushed diamonds do work, I still prefer gentler (and cheaper!) exfoliators for skin.

I guess in a broad sense, we can classify exfoliators into mechanical and chemical exfoliators. There are many skincare brands that contain granules that help exfoliate the skin. Some use larger beads or granules like jojoba beads to help scrub off the top layer of skin. Chemical exfoliators include AHA (alpha hydroxy-acids). These were widely promoted in the US as anti-ageing exfoliators. However, brown skin does not age as easily as white skin, and I prefer to avoid chemicals and stick to natural skincare techniques as much as possible.

The natural exfoliator I have detailed below works well. And, let's not forget, AHA are derived from fruit acids.

> **Recipe for home-made exfoliator**
>
> Take equal parts of papaya and pineapple and blend with an equal part of coarse sea salt. You can use this as a facial scrub. Papaya and pineapple contain enzymes that act as good chemical exfoliants.

Why does exfoliation work? What is the advantage in taking off the outermost layer of skin when it happens naturally anyway? Essentially, cells migrate from deeper layers of skin to the outer layer. As they migrate, they get dehydrated and become rougher due to the presence of a dry protein called keratin. There is a constant process of shedding cells in the outer layer. This layer is important as it gives our skin some protection – sort of making concrete rougher on the outer walls, so that people cannot stick notices on them. But as we get older, this natural process of shedding of cells becomes less frequent and erratic. Cells are not shed evenly and at an equal rate from all parts of the skin, leading to an uneven appearance. When the sun falls on such uneven areas, they can tan differently, leading to pigmentation and the appearance of spots. Exfoliation can remove the outer cells evenly and reveal younger-looking cells beneath the skin. Needless to say, periodic exfoliation (ideally once or twice a week) will make your skin look younger.

I had explained earlier how skin pores can become clogged or end up as blackheads, and how exfoliating scrubs also help scrub off any residue sitting within the openings of the pores. There was a theory that using a toner after an exfoliator makes these pores look smaller. But I used my fluorescence spectrometer to check this out and I did not come away convinced that it was right.

However, brown skin is smooth and not as prone to roughness as white skin. I see many white patients with severe sun-damaged skin and if you run your fingers over the skin, it feels dry and rough. There are areas that we medically refer to as hyper-keratotic, i.e., having excess build-up of keratin that makes the skin feel horny like a lizard. But in brown skin, we rarely see this unless the person has a skin disease like psoriasis. As brown skin is generally smooth, over-exfoliating the skin will make it more sensitive and also lead to redness. I have developed a micro-granular exfoliator for brown skin, so that the exfoliating effect is very gentle. I only recommend exfoliating once a week. If someone has excessive oiliness of skin, this can be increased to twice a week. For those with clogged pores and acne, I sometimes recommend daily exfoliation, but with a gentle exfoliator.

In India, especially in the north, besan or chickpea flour is often used as a gentle exfoliator to scrub skin. In south India, dried moong dal also makes for a gentle exfoliator. In traditional Indian recipes, moong dal was mixed with turmeric; the latter has antibacterial properties and hence helps with acne. We also know that turmeric contains a compound called curcumin that helps reduce the effects of photo-ageing, i.e., pigmentation and skin damage. However, of late, turmeric has fallen out of favour with the young as they don't want to look yellow.

Key points

- Skin naturally sheds outer layers; however, this process slows down with age.

- Exfoliation is removal of outer layer of skin gently to reveal underlying younger skin.

- In brown skin type, I do not recommend exfoliating more than once or twice a week.

- Home-made mechanical exfoliator: sea salt.

- Home-made natural chemical exfoliator: papaya and pineapple in equal parts blended together.

6

Alcoholic v. Non-alcoholic Toners

*What is a toner? Does toning skin means making it firmer,
like toning muscles does? Surely one cannot exercise facial
skin?*

...

In beauty salons, aestheticians tend to cleanse the skin and
exfoliate. Once the outer layer of skin has been exfoliated, they
follow up with a toner to make the skin feel clean and refreshed.

A skin toner is essentially used to hydrate skin and remove
oil, make-up and other residues. However, many experts
even believe that using a good cleanser in itself will remove
most residues, and that an astringent toner is not needed.
(Technically speaking, an astringent constricts bodily tissues
and therefore makes pores smaller.) It was also felt that toners
reduce the size of pores and make them much smaller. I have
not found this to be true in my research on non-alcoholic
toners. While a toner probably removes residues, hydrates
skin and makes it feel lively, in brown skin, the pores are well
developed – especially in the T-zone – and won't open and
close like a window. This was why many toners contained
alcohol, which does indeed close pores – the dehydration
that alcohol causes leads to the shrinkage of tissues, which in
turn makes the pores close. But we know that dehydration is

bad, and that brown skin is especially prone to dryness on the cheeks. Therefore, I do not recommend alcohol-based toners for brown skin. One of the main reasons to avoid alcoholic toners in any skin type is that it strips skin of natural oils and can lead to dryness. Of course, many people do not like to use alcohol anyway – even if Russians swear by their pure vodka as a good toner. Might be good for their skin type, who knows? I haven't studied their skin in detail yet.

It is important to cleanse skin daily. But I would recommend exfoliation only once or twice a week. On days that you use an exfoliator, you can remove residues left behind by using a toner. When I developed an alcohol-free hydrating toner, it was mainly because I wanted a product that could be used by itself as a hydrating skin agent. Whenever I have travelled through India, especially in summer, I have found that this toner makes my face feel more 'awake', and when the weather is very humid and the skin is full of sweat and residue, toning does help refresh skin. However, while toning is important after exfoliating, as the exfoliating scrub would have left some residue, it is not necessary to use a toner every day.

In this book, I will list some old home-made skincare recipes for you. Here, I will give you two recipes – one with alcohol and the other without. The former was given by a Russian model from her grandmother's skincare recipe and contains (no surprise there!) vodka.

> **Recipes for skin toner**
>
> Blend half a cup of pureed cucumbers with a quarter-cup of vodka. Dab this toner on your face using a ball of cotton.
>
> Here is a traditional Indian skin toner: boil mint leaves in water to make mint tea; then allow to cool. Mix one cup of this cold mint tea with two tablespoons of lemon juice. Dab across face using balls of cotton.

Key points

- Toning skin helps remove residue.
- While toning after exfoliating is good, toning is not needed every day.
- Toners may contain alcohol, although I prefer alcohol-free toners.
- Home-made alcohol-free toner: mint tea and lemon; home-made toner with alcohol: vodka and cucumber.
- I recommend only alcohol-free toners for brown and Asian skin types.

7

Soaps v. Cleansers

You say that one needs to cleanse skin daily, but exfoliate/ tone once or twice a week. On the other hand, you say that using soap is harmful for the skin. How does one cleanse skin daily without using soap?

...

Virtually all dermatologists and skin researchers will tell you that soap is bad for skin as it washes off natural oils. Yet, soaps make up a large volume of supermarket and shop shelves. This is often confusing to people as many soaps claim to be 'moisturizing' or 'antibacterial soaps'.

So does one need soap? All I can say is that one definitely needs a foaming cleanser to wash areas like armpits and groins. These areas of the body contain hair that are different from sweat glands in other bodily areas.

The problem with soap is to do with pH. A quick trip down memory lane to high-school chemistry class reminds us that 'pH' means 'potential of hydrogen'. As pH is a log scale, for every unit change, there is a tenfold increase or decrease in the number of hydrogen atoms present. When pH is neutral, a substance is neither acidic nor alkaline, i.e., its H+ (acidic) and OH– (alkaline) ions are balanced. Therefore, when H+ and OH– combine we get water, which is neutral, i.e., it has a pH of 7.

The pH of human blood is regulated by the body in the range of 7.35 to 7.45. However, the pH of adult human skin is 5.5. Why the difference? When a baby is born, its pH is around 7, and this progressively turns more acidic in order to protect the tender infant skin from infections. When a child reaches puberty, due to hormonal changes, the skin is more susceptible to bacterial and fungal infections (from acne and increased sweating, etc.). In some ways, the development of bodily hair at puberty is a skin defence mechanism; as more sebaceous glands become active, it leads to more oil (sebum) production. This combination of oil and sweat decreases the pH of skin to 5.5 – an acidic environment that is inherently hostile to bacteria. Some refer to this change in skin at puberty as the development of an 'acid mantle'.

This has some practical implications. Traditional soaps are generally very alkaline, with a pH of 9–11. Using soap, therefore, disrupts the acid mantle. This is why dermatologists usually recommend (so do I) soap-free cleansers or 'pH neutral' cleansers.

Essentially, there are two types of sweat glands – apocrine glands that are found in armpits and groin areas, and eccrine glands that are found in the rest of the body, including the face. The eccrine glands essentially open directly onto the surface of the skin. Therefore, the sweat is 'fresh' and does not smell. However, in areas like the groin and armpits, the apocrine glands have a slightly different anatomy. They open into hair follicles before they reach the surface of the skin. Further, these glands produce sweat that contains more fat, is thicker and more prone to bacterial contamination as these areas are generally covered by clothing and not aired as often as other parts of the body. This is why sweat in the armpits and groin can produce body odour as well as mark clothing. It is therefore important to wash these areas with soap or foaming cleansers. But in other parts of body this is unnecessary.

In animals like dogs, most of the glands are apocrine, hence the 'dog smell'. These glands in dogs are used as 'pheromones' to attract mates and have hormonal functions. Eccrine glands or conventional sweat glands are not found on the dog except on the nose – which is why dogs cool down by panting and not by sweating. This is why it is dangerous to cover the mouth of a dog or muzzle it when it is hot as the dog can reach dangerously, even fatally, high body temperatures. I have found this interesting not just as a dog lover, but as a student of evolution of skin and sweat glands.

To return to what we were discussing for the face, by and large clean water should suffice, unless one is using heavy make-up (when you will need make-up removers specific to the type of product you use). Firstly, do not use too cold or too hot water as both can damage skin capillaries and can result in a reddish appearance of the face or broken blood vessels. It is important to wash the face at night so that it is clean; this will also prevent bacteria from colonizing your skin overnight. Interestingly, this is where 'cold cream' originated, as French women traditionally used cold cream to wipe the face at night without water. In the morning, just a splash of lukewarm water will do.

People in the West traditionally use a washcloth and fill the sink or washbasin with water and wash using a cloth. In India, we tend to use running tap water. In Asian conditions, running tap water is actually better. For one, using the 'pooled' water in a sink is not ideal because of the risk of bacterial or microbial contamination. Secondly, hard water, which is found in many parts of India, has higher levels of dissolved minerals like calcium and magnesium and, therefore, is not ideal for cleansing skin. It is better to wash the face by splashing water on it, rather than soak facial skin in hard water.

Hard water per se is not bad for skin. But when cleansing products or soap are used with hard water, sometimes they form 'scum', which is more difficult to clean using pooled water.

> **Galen's recipe for cold cream**
>
> Use six tablespoons of olive oil and six tablespoons of distilled water mixed with half a cup of grated (then melted and cooled) beeswax. Rose petals were used to give it fragrance.

While washing one's face with water, do remember to massage the facial skin against gravity, i.e., use strokes directed upwards and outwards. This not only stimulates facial circulation but also aids cleansing of clogged pores.

It is said that Galen, the Greek, first developed cold creams. As a physician in ancient Rome (Galen actually practised as a doctor and healer in Rome, although he was originally of Greek descent, and is often referred to as a Roman), he was asked to tend to the wounds of gladiators. While developing wound-care creams, he began formulating facial cold creams and moisturizers.

If I were to make a home-made cold cream to use at night, I would prefer to use pressed rose hip oil from the seeds of a rose bush. Traditionally used in South America, this is good for brown skin and has good Vitamin C content; also, it has a lower acne-causing effect than olive oil. In Morocco, the equivalent is argan oil, which is similarly used to make cold creams and skin products. In India, if we cold-press sunflower seeds to extract oil, it can also be used to make a cold cream. Cold creams can be used on the face and wiped off. In the morning, wash with running lukewarm tap water.

> **Recipe for home-made cold cream**
>
> Boil a large pan of water and float a smaller metal bowl in it containing half a cup of beeswax, six tablespoons of pressed oil (you choose!) and six tablespoons of distilled water. Stir until the wax is dissolved and the mixture liquefies. Then take off heat and allow to cool in a glass jar. It will have the consistency of a soothing balm.

Key points

- Cleansing is important, especially at night, to wash off accumulated dust, smoke and pollutants from modern city lifestyles.

- Cleansing also unclogs pores.

- While cleansing, use lukewarm water and wash your face upwards and outwards.

- Home-made cold cream can be used as a cleanser: beeswax and olive oil or rose hip oil and distilled water.

8

Sugar v. Fat

I've heard people say that eating sweets is bad for the skin. I've also read that it makes no difference what you eat. Do you believe diet makes a difference? ...

About five or six years ago, Colleen, a Canadian friend (now in her mid-forties) told me that she had finally figured out why she was getting breakouts of acne on her face. She had consulted numerous dermatologists and they could not fix her problem. In the end, she gave up dairy for a month and found that her skin had cleared up. Why did you not tell me to stop eating dairy products? she asked me. I felt pretty useless as a doctor and skin researcher at not having diagnosed her skin condition.

I remember telling her that while some people had a specific allergy to dairy, which usually manifested as dermatitis or eczema-like rashes in early childhood, I did not know about any specific link between acne in adulthood and dairy products. She had switched to soy milk in her forties. It is true that soybean has been shown to have some benefits: it contains plant oestrogen and could have positive effects around menopause, and certain soy extracts have been used topically as skin creams (due to soybeans containing genistein, which reduce the effects of UV damage). But there has been no conclusive study showing the benefits of soy specifically to do with skin when eaten in the diet.

However, in 2009, a review evaluated the published literature on the association between diet and acne risk and severity. Its authors showed that dairy products and high-glycaemic-index foods increased the risk for acne. So before we doctors had any published scientific evidence, Colleen had diagnosed herself.

Similarly, there will be many people who find that a certain food aggravates their skin and as I tell my patients – you are the best guide as to what is good for you. That said, I will discuss diet and skin in a holistic manner here and give dietary advice for general skin health.

The commonest thing teenagers ask me is if chocolate can exacerbate acne. Until recently, there was no scientific evidence that eating too much chocolate worsened acne. However, in February 2011, another paper presented at the American Academy of Dermatology meeting showed a link between acne and chocolate consumption, especially in males. So there is evidence that if your skin is prone to acne, eating chocolate may be bad (especially in young men).

Let us look at some specific foods that have been shown to have effects on the skin:

FISH OIL

Eating oily fish like salmon, or consuming fish oil capsules have been known to be beneficial for the skin. Fish oil supplementation has shown to reduce the effects of UVB damage, although it did not show any specific beneficial effects on the skin lipid layer.

Red wine/dark grapes

Resveratrol, an antioxidant polyphenol in red wine, has been
the subject of huge medical and scientific interest in recent
years due to its various effects. Recent evidence suggests
that it has beneficial effects on cardiac health. Of course,
excessive alcohol drinking dehydrates the skin and has the
opposite effect, not to mention several other harmful effects.
For example, when we biopsy skin for testing, before we cut
up specimens, the samples are repeatedly washed in serially
higher concentrations of alcohol to remove the water content
so they can be sliced and mounted on slides. Alcohol is
perhaps the greatest dehydrating agent (as I tell my Australian
students after a night out on the 'turps' watching 'footy' in
Aussie pubs), so it is best not to drink more than a glass or two
of red wine at night. Remember to drink a glass of water for
each glass of wine. This is also the reason I prefer alcohol-free
toners as they tend to dehydrate the skin, thereby nullifying
the hydrating effects of the toners. One needs to drink a lot of
red wine to get enough resveratrol, which leads to other bad
effects of alcohol on liver and skin. If you want high doses
of resveratrol in your system you might have to pop a pill,
or even better drink dark non-alcoholic grape juice or eat
dark grapes.

Oranges/citrus fruit

Vitamin C is extremely important for the skin. In fact, the
best skincare advice is to eat enough Vitamin C and also use
products containing Vitamin C or citrus extracts on the skin.
When I first developed my skincare range, Mikanis, it was
because I remember seeing villagers in south India rubbing
orange peels on their skins before going out on the fields. That
led me to research the matter further and to develop unique
extracts, which in turn led to developing the entire range.

Eating two slices of oranges a day can give you your daily requirement of Vitamin C.

One of the interesting things with Vitamin C is this: I was testing my Vitamin C serums on my clients. We could see (using our skin scanners) improvement in their skin after using the serums. We could also see the benefit in eating Vitamin C in fruit form (citrus fruits). As many dermatologists prescribe high-dose Vitamin C, which is the synthetic version, I tested this to find *no skin* benefit. In the beginning I thought this was an error in my analyses or scanner. But now we know that this phenomenon is well known as the xenobiotic metabolism – the body recognizes the synthetic version as alien. Oral Vitamin C tablets may work on other internal organs, but on the skin's surface, there is no visible benefit – we see benefits of Vitamin C on skin when used as serums or consumed via fruit. Therefore, natural is best; as with foods, the less processed the better.

FOOD SOURCES

Vitamin D is also important and I will discuss this in detail later. Vitamin D is found in fish oils and fortified foods and is produced by the skin on sun exposure.

Tomatoes have been mentioned for their antioxidant effect. While it is true that tomatoes have good antioxidant properties, I remember Uncle Bobby (to whom this book is dedicated) used to tell his patients to avoid tomatoes if they had pigmentation around the mouth.

There are several foods that are said to have specific skin benefits, but I have restricted myself to mentioning foods that scientific studies prove to be beneficial to skin, as opposed to general health.

However, the skin is the body's largest organ and one cannot have poor health and have good skin. If people see me and remark that I look much younger than my years, it is because my diet is varied and healthy, I do not eat processed food and I consume enough vitamins C and D. I am surprised how many people in India eat processed foods, i.e., food manufactured and packaged with added salt and preservatives. I cannot remember the last time I ate salted chips from a packet. It is not just to set a good example – if you are healthy and lead a balanced lifestyle (everything in moderation), your skin feels and looks good. I have been a medical doctor for over twenty-five years and have never lost a working day due to illness. I didn't think this was a big deal, but the more I have mentioned this, the more I have come to realize that it might be.

In general, it is essential to eat plenty of fruits and vegetables. Most people in India eat vegetables aplenty, but we tend to overcook them. The more raw our fruit and vegetable consumption, the better, because cooking often removes nutrients. It is also advisable to avoid oily curries and deep-fried dishes.

Refined sugar, or simple sugar, does not need to be broken down, so it gets converted to fat unless it is burned off immediately (and therefore has a high glycaemic index). Indian sweets are full of refined sugar. Sugars in general can be refined or complex. Complex sugars have a lower glycaemic index. They need to be broken down, like in rice or pasta, and they are all right in the diet, as long as one undertakes some form of daily exercise. The good old basmati rice has the lowest glycaemic index of all white rice varieties. Otherwise, brown rice is the best. In general, it is best to avoid refined sugars like in sweets as much as possible. Of course an occasional treat is fine, if only to limit craving.

While turmeric was widely used on the skin in south India, scientific studies have now shown that it works against stress on the skin. To clarify, stress and sun damage cause the same antioxidant cellular pathways to be activated. Foods that help reduce the stress response, like turmeric or broccoli, also help skin. Turmeric has shown beneficial health effects against dementia and neurological conditions; it also has antibacterial properties, which is perhaps why it was used to reduce acne. Green tea, grapeseed and licorice have also shown antioxidant effects, but more specifically have some properties that reduce the redness of skin.

Key points

- Eat raw foods and avoid processed foods or salt-added packet foods.

- Dark-coloured fruits and vegetables are better, and raw or juiced is better than cooked.

- If cooking with oil, avoid frying and use olive oil or rice bran oil.

- Nuts are good, especially almonds, walnuts and Brazil nuts.

- Vitamin C is excellent for skin both topically and also when taken internally as citrus fruits.

- It is good to get thirty minutes of sun exposure twice a day, outside peak hours (12–4 p.m.) so that the skin is not Vitamin D deficient. Make sure you get enough vitamins C and D.

- Recent evidence does link acne and chocolate in the diet, especially in young men; avoid refined sugar and junk food.

- In some people, acne can be aggravated by dairy products.

9

Alcohol v. Water

You've just mentioned alcohol is bad for skin. My husband drinks a fair bit, especially when he goes out with friends, and I drink too, in moderation. What problems does alcohol pose for the skin? Does quantity matter? ...

Alcohol has adverse effects on the liver and can cause hypertension, as we already know. 'The French Paradox', which made red wine popular worldwide, is that the French drink red wine but also have low heart disease in spite of high butter content in their diets as well as a propensity to smoke. This led to research that suggested the benefits of moderate alcohol (especially red wine) intake. The benefits of resveratrol are now well known. However, as I mentioned earlier, alcohol is a strong dehydrating agent and has been found to have specific negative effects on skin.

There are a few specific problems that excessive intake of alcohol can cause. Most males who drink heavily are hyper-oestrogenic, i.e., develop high oestrogen (female hormone) levels and this can lead to gynaecomastia ('man-boobs' or 'moobs'). Seeing that you are concerned about your husband's drinking, if you mention this fact to him, it might put him off drinking too much!

The other issue with alcohol is the calorific content. In general, a standard alcoholic drink has the calorie content of a pizza slice or a piece of cake. When young figure-conscious women friends go out drinking, I jokingly ask them later how many cakes they have had.

Studies on Asians, including Indians, have shown that up to 50 per cent of Asians lack the ability to make a particular enzyme, aldehyde dehydrogenase (that breaks down molecules of acetaldehyde; acetaldehyde is an intermediate product during yeast fermentation and therefore found in alcohol), leading to an accumulation of acetaldehyde after alcohol consumption. This makes brown skin prone to redness and flushing over a longer period of time and leads to rashes on cheeks, like the condition called rosacea, even in dark skin. This could also account for the higher levels of liver disease in Asian alcoholics. The higher incidence of liver ailments is not connected with body weight – a theory that probably comes from the fact that Indians are, by and large, not as big as European or Pacific Island races – but is due to the lower levels of the enzyme that detoxifies alcohol.

While it is known that alcohol can cause broken blood vessels, more recently, several studies have shown a strong link between alcohol and psoriasis, which causes thick plaque-like rashes on the body. Two major studies published in the USA, which were conducted by following 82,869 women for fourteen years, showed that consumption of more than 2 or 3 alcoholic beverages per week was a significant risk factor for new onset of psoriasis. In males too, excess alcohol consumption appears to be a risk factor for the development and increased activity of psoriasis and resistance to treatment. While drinking alcohol, it is important to drink water to combat dehydration.

Key points

- Alcohol in moderation has shown cardiovascular benefits.

- Alcohol, however, is a strong dehydrating agent and also has specific harmful effects on skin.

- Alcohol causes redness and rosacea. The strong dehydrating effect of alcohol also worsens dermatitis/eczema where skin hydration is the most important part of therapy.

- Many Asians specifically lack an enzyme that metabolizes alcohol and this leads to higher incidence of bad skin and liver problems in drinkers. It is best to limit alcohol consumption to under three drinks a week.

- Alcohol specifically worsens conditions like psoriasis and also makes it more resistant to treatment.

10

Moisturizers v. Acne

My friend says that every time she uses moisturizers her acne gets worse. Can this happen? You've just been telling us about the importance of skin moisturizing. What's the solution?

This is not actually a myth. Like I said earlier, brown skin is especially prone to oiliness in the T-zone region because of the deeper and wider pores there, which secrete more oil. As I alluded to earlier, using ingredients like cocoa butter on the skin can cause it to clog pores and indeed cause breakouts. The fat in the cocoa butter acts like the fat in sebum and it blocks pores. There is a particular bacterium implicated in acne called propionibacterium, which tends to break down the fat clogging the pores. The result: inflamed acne. This is why low-dose antibiotics have a long-term use in acne management.

It is important to check the ingredients of moisturizers and sunscreens, and ensure they are not comedogenic, i.e., not likely to clog pores. Studies have implicated many ingredients as being comedogenic: isopropyl myristate, cocoa butter, lanolin, butyl stearate, stearyl alcohol and oleic acid. For Asian/tropical conditions and Asian/Latino skin, I advise light moisturizers and also lower-SPF sunscreens. Some natural oils like olive oil, almond oil and coconut oil are also comedogenic, especially on the face.

When an acne-prone person has a facial, he or she can sometimes develop acne after the facial. This is because the massaging action might have caused an inflammatory reaction of the hair follicle wall. This in turn causes swelling and the resultant inflammation leads to bacterial colonization and pimple formation. Or they may not develop typical acne with inflammation, but end up with small bumps on the forehead. These are small closed comedones. If you are developing little bumps on the forehead, you need to look closely at the moisturizers or make-up you are using. Another cause could be hair gel or pomade that is clogging forehead pores on the hairline near the forehead. For acne-prone individuals it is important to use an acne-cleanser and an exfoliator. These cleansers generally have an ingredient that exfoliates the follicle and also kills the bacteria associated with acne. Anti-acne skin cleansers and cosmetics typically contain either salicylic acid or benzoyl peroxide. Both of these are FDA-approved drugs for acne treatment.

However, it is important that if acne is not controlled with cosmetics, the afflicted person must consult a dermatologist and start on an acne eradication programme early because brown skin is especially prone to acne scarring and pigmentation.

Key points

- Some cosmetic ingredients can indeed worsen acne.

- Acne-prone individuals should be cautious about getting facials done, especially if they have a function or event in the next three or four days.

- Some comedogenic ingredients, i.e., ingredients that can cause breakouts, are cocoa butter, lanolin, and coconut and olive oil.

- Look out for and avoid these ingredients in cosmetics: isopropyl myristate, cocoa butter, lanolin, butyl stearate, stearyl alcohol and oleic acid.

- Acne-prone individuals should use both acne skin cleansers and topical acne gels.

- If acne is not controlled with cosmetics, seek medical help.

- Brown skin is especially prone to acne scarring, so it is important to avoid products that can worsen acne.

11

Oil-in-water v. Water-in-oil

I live in New Delhi and, especially in winter, my skin starts to peel and gets really dry. I was considering buying a tub of cocoa or shea butter as I've seen them in several international cosmetic chain stores. But you have said they can cause breakouts. I'm confused. What should I do about my dry skin then?

    ...

Yes, even though brown skin is prone to oiliness around the nose and forehead, dryness on the body is common to most skin types. It is therefore important to moisturize. I've already stated that lighter moisturizers are better for brown skin, unless one has a skin condition exacerbated by dryness like eczema.

There are two ways you can stop the oily layer of the skin from drying out or getting damaged. One method is to use a protective layer – the 'shield' method – using emollients, that is the use of petroleum jelly to prevent moisture loss. Especially when the skin is very dry and has reached 'breaking point', these are ideal. Rather than being quickly absorbed, they sit like a shield on top of the outer later.

Natural home-made emollients are sunflower seed oil and olive oil. In India, sandalwood oil has been used as an emollient because of its fragrance. But while oils feel nicer on the skin than petroleum jelly, which tends to be sticky (as do cocoa or shea butter, which are heavy), they are more easily absorbed by the skin and therefore lose some of the shield function. Oils are better used when you notice your skin is dry, rather than when your skin has already become scratched, broken or irritated. In fact, they are best used before a bath or shower.

Some synthetic emollients are silicone-based. But considering silica is found in sand, their origins are natural, and so some people regard silicone as a natural ingredient. In fact, various sea sponges as well as micro-organisms secrete skeletal structures made of silica. In 2010, I travelled to Iceland for the Nordic Plastic Surgical Congress. I was presenting my new skin-grafting technique, the 'Halo Graft', to an international group of plastic surgeons. As part of the conference activities, we were taken to the famed Icelandic hot pool, the Blue Lagoon. The water there is full of silica, minerals and algae that are supposed to have great healing properties, especially for psoriasis. Silica rocks dot the banks of the lagoon and everyone uses the whitish powder on the rocks as ointment for the skin. I applied some to my face and soon I looked like a beetroot. I always tell my patients to test for allergies by applying a test dose of cream behind their ears or on their arms! My face remained red for a few days before returning to normal.

What I like about silicone is that it is non-toxic, spreads nicely as a shield, moisturizes skin, is lightweight and ideal for brown skin as it does not clog pores. Some of my products for brown skin use silicone. A moisturizer containing silicone will feel silky on the skin – in the cosmetics trade, we refer to this as having more 'slip'.

If you cannot have a shield around the skin, you'd want the skin to stop moisture from escaping. This is the 'retention' method: keeping the skin moist using ingredients referred to as humectants. These ingredients are hygroscopic, absorb water and bind to skin, thereby retaining moisture. I commonly prescribe glycerol in cetomacrogol (which is a surfactant-rich cream) as a humectant; both glycerine and sorbital have a good humectant effect and reduce moisture loss. As these are absorbed by the skin, glycerine or glycerol generally does not clog pores or cause pimples to break out.

In your case, I'd say it would be important to use a humectant, but not too much emollient unless you are using a lightweight one like silicone that will not clog your pores. If you use an oil-based product, you may not get enough protection for broken skin, and petroleum jelly would be too heavy for hot conditions.

I'll take a moment here to explain the pharmaceutical formulation. In essence, you make moisturizers either by using oil-in-water or water-in-oil. Oil-in-water contains mainly water in which the oil is virtually dissolved due to the abundance of water content. These make up the bulk of formulations because they are less greasy. However, the water evaporates in hot conditions, making them less effective. Water-in-oil is mostly oil in which water has been dissolved by dilution. They make the skin shiny and feel warmer. This is why many brown-skinned people feel that moisturizers make them sweat. It is because water-in-oil formulations are not good as day creams in Latino and Asian hot conditions. My own moisturizers for brown skin use light silicone, which makes for an excellent moisturizer in hot and warm climes.

Once you've made a water-in-oil or an oil-in-water formulation, the next step is customizing them for different body areas.

As a general guide to the composition of moisturizers, body lotions are made up of 10 to 15 per cent in the oil phase and 75 to 85 per cent in the water phase, which is why they are lotions and more runny. The remaining 5 per cent are humectants (as discussed earlier) like glycerine.

Hand creams, for example, contain 20–40 per cent in the oil phase and 40–60 per cent in the water phase and 15 per cent humectants, making them a lot thicker. Hand creams are the thickest of all formulations because they need to penetrate the extra cuticle layer found in palms and soles. For people prone to dark circles around the eyes, I recommend a heavy water-in-oil moisturizer at night. As those areas do not have a lot of pores, heavy moisturizers are safe to use.

When skin gets dry in brown conditions, it can also get itchy. Not taking showers more than once a day, or keeping them short can help retain moisture. Again, it is better to have water at room temperature or lukewarm in tropical conditions and avoid soap (except in the armpits and the groin area). If you are using any oil, it is better applied before a shower or bath. It is also important to moisturize before taking a flight as the recycled air and air conditioning are extremely drying. I normally recommend moisturizing the face, especially around the eyes just before flying. For flights longer than four hours, I'd advise reapplying the moisturizer. This dryness is often more pronounced in brown skin type around the eyes and leads to the appearance of dark circles or puffiness.

Key points

- Avoid showers that are too hot or too cold.
- Keep showers lukewarm and short, and if possible limit to one a day.
- If using oil, apply before a shower.
- Emollients (e.g., petroleum jelly) protect skin like a shield, but can clog pores.
- Humectants (e.g., glycerine) prevent skin from losing moisture and don't generally clog pores.
- Silicone is a good lightweight emollient for brown skin as it does not clog pores.

12

Alpha v. Beta (Hydroxy-acids)

I have heard that facial peels are not good for brown skin. Is that true? I also see a lot of different places advertising different types of peels, and I am not sure which you'd recommend for brown skin. Also, I've been told that facial peeling is the best way to improve my skin colour and make it lighter. And I keep hearing of alpha and beta hydroxy-acids in the context of peels. What are these?

...

I understand the need to deal with what we medically term dyschromias, i.e., uneven skin colouring or patches, but urge my clients to be happy with the skin colour they were born with (and not seek lightening of skin, because however much cosmetics may lighten your skin, your skin type and all of the associated problems and advantages remain the same). But a contour or colour defect, i.e., a small depressed or raised mark on the face, is more noticeable because light casts a shadow over the face. Similarly, a localized patch of mismatched skin colour is more likely to stand out to an observer. And these issues obviously cause distress and need treatment.

I will start by explaining superficial chemical peels as these are the ones you will come across in most places. Nowadays, many products advertise alpha hydroxy-acids or AHAs. Many of these agents have natural origins. Ancient Greeks, Romans and Egyptians used alpha hydroxy-acids found in various fruits and plants in ancient times, and there are many detailed reports on their use. Beta hydroxy-acids or BHAs have also been used in facial peels; however, these are lipophilic, i.e., they target and can damage the skin's vital oil layer and therefore are best used only when excessive oil production is a problem (as on acne-prone skin).

So, many of the names you see in advertisements for facial peels, like glycolic peels, are acids with natural origins.

The humble willow, which produces BHA, was also the original source of the wonder drug aspirin. Hippocrates, the father of modern medicine, described using willow bark as remedies for headaches and fevers.

> **Plants/fruits that contain alpha hydroxy-acids**
> - Sugar cane: glycolic acid
> - Sour milk or yoghurt/curd: lactic acid
> - Citrus fruits like lemons/oranges: citric acid
> - Grapes: tartaric acid
> - Apples: malic acid
>
> **Plants/fruits that contain beta hydroxy-acids**
> - Willow tree (from the bark of the tree): salicylic acid

In my view, aggressive facial peeling and repeated treatments are not ideal for brown skin because they could cause unevenness of skin tone and colour, leaving you unhappy with the results. The first rule of medicine is *primum non nocere* (first, do no harm).

The real issue with facial peels is that, to be really effective, they need to cause irritation of the outer layer of skin to provoke an irritant dermatitis. Managing this dermatitis carefully is what leads to the desired appearance. However, brown skin is especially prone to uneven skin tone and hence one needs to manage it carefully both before and after treatment. When using chemicals, one needs to titrate them carefully and treat slowly over many months or years.

If you need more aggressive treatment, it is best done in consultation with a good cosmetic dermatologist, so that the treatments and drugs can be tailored for your skin type and specific needs.

To answer your question, chemical peels work just as the name suggests: the theory is that by peeling off the outer layer of skin, we are allowing new skin to grow more healthily. The fruits I mentioned earlier, like lemons, apples and grapes, and dairy products like yoghurt, have all been used as home-care remedies and you can try these if you like. They are unlikely to have side effects because the concentration will not be enough to make your skin peel aggressively. In essence, the depth of skin peeling depends on the amount used, the pressure used by the person doing the peel and the length of time that the solution is left on the skin.

Of the acids I have discussed, glycolic acid is the most potent peeling agent, and, in 5–10 per cent of people, will cause hyperpigmentation, or darkening of skin over peeled areas, which gets worse on sun exposure. Unfortunately, we brown-skinned people are more prone to this post-inflammatory pigmentation. However, glycolic acid is often used in concentrations of 10–70 per cent. It is important that the acid is neutralized with either water or bicarbonate while doing the peel, especially in concentrations over 30 per cent.

Other than the alpha hydroxy-acids we discussed above, certain synthetic chemicals are also used to remove pigmentation. These are hydroquinone and topical retinoids like tretinoin. While topical retinoids can help pigmentation, if a patient has been on oral retinoids for acne or other conditions, no peels or skin surgery must be done for a year. This is because if someone has been on an oral retinoid like roaccutane, isotane or a similar agent, surgical scars can be more prone to becoming hypertrophic (thick and unsightly). Further, those using retinoids must also avoid the sun, because these can induce photosensitivity.

If any chemical is used to induce a peel in too high concentrations in brown skin, one runs the risk of the skin becoming too light and end up with leucoderma- or vitiligo-like white patches. Since ancient times, Indians have feared white skin patches because of its association with leprosy and the associated stigma (even though leprosy is amongst the least contagious of all diseases). Ancient literature refers to these white patches as shveta kushta or 'white leprosy'. The late pop star Michael Jackson is a sad example of over-treatment. I've seen many patients who have used hydroquinone to lighten pigmented areas develop unsightly white patches. Personally, I avoid using or prescribing hydroquinone. There have also been reports linking hydroquinone with cancer and while it is still widely used in the US, it is avoided in Australia and NZ. As an alternative to hydroquinone in cosmetics, many berry extracts have been used as skin-whitening agents. The active agent that lightens skin in mulberry and bearberry is arbutin.

Cosmetics containing azelaic acids are often advertised for skin discolouration. Azelaic acid is found in wheat, rye and barley, and I've seen 'beer facials' advertised in parts of Europe. Another acid used in peels that originated in Japan (like India, Japan is another country with an obsession for skin-whitening products) is kojic acid, which is a byproduct of the malting and fermentation process for sake, Japanese rice wine. But as kojic acid is unstable and cannot be used effectively in cosmetics (even if they are so advertised), it is often just used for 'sake facials'. It's good to remember that any facial using alcohol will need a good hydrating moisturizer afterwards.

In summary, if you are considering a facial peel to reduce pigmentation, you must be aware that skin may not lighten evenly, making matters worse. If your skin has an even tone

Recipe for home-made alpha hydroxy-acid facial pack

Use citrus fruits like lemons or oranges (citric acid), grapes (tartaric acid) or apples (malic acid).

Blend or puree each fruit (one cup of a fruit of your choice from the list above). Add honey (two tablespoons) or aloe vera gel to help retain skin moisture. Many people use plain unflavoured gelatine to help bind the fruit puree/blend (one packet dissolved in hot green tea and then cooled). Refrigerate for twenty minutes. Allow to thicken and then leave on face for twenty minutes.

Yoghurt (50 per cent) and sugar cane (50 per cent) mixture (lactic acid and glycolic acid), one cup. Add two tablespoons of honey.

and you are looking for overall lightening, you may have a slightly lower risk, i.e., a facial peel is not ideal to treat localized pigmentation (better seek medical advice). If you're going in for a superficial chemical peel using glycolic acid, ensure that it is neutralized; opt for the most gentle and mildest concentration to begin with.

Lastly, many people I know swear by the facials they put together; so of course you can try your own recipe.

Green tea has shown skin benefits and most home-made AHA treatments use a fruit containing AHA and use gelatine dissolved in green tea to help make up the skin treatment.

I personally do not recommend hydroquinone in brown skin types, as other than the risks of toxicity I have seen a higher risk of white patches resulting from its use.

Key points

- Brown skin runs the risk of hyperpigmentation and atypical skin tone after a facial peel.

- After a facial peel, avoid sun exposure for a few weeks – just using sunblock may not be enough.

- If you are on a retinoid or have been in the past year, you will have an increased risk of scarring.

- Glycolic acid is the most commonly used alpha hydroxy-acid (AHA) but is most potent, so it is important that it is neutralized while doing the peel.

- Salicylic acid is the most commonly used beta hydroxy-acid (BHA) but this affects the lipid layer of skin, so it is best reserved for those with acne or oily skin.

13

Sensitive Skin v. Pigmentation

You have spoken of classifying brown skin into three types using your 'SPA classification'. Can you explain this further? And how do I know where I fit in? My skin seems to react to most suncreams and skin products? ...

This is a good question. My classification is based on the fact that brown skin tends to suffer from three common complaints: Sensitivity (S), Pigmentation (P) and Acne (A). Very rarely do I hear my Indian, Asian or Latino patients speak about ageing or wrinkles, but pigmentation and sensitive skin are at the top of the complaint list for the over-thirty age group, and acne and sensitive skin for the under-thirty lot.

At different stages of life the predominant concerns might be different. In my patients with white skin, the three concerns are wrinkles, skin cancer or growths and pigmentation. Therefore, my SPA classification helps the brown clients plan their daily skincare regimen based on what their needs are at a given point in time.

The classification is simple: if redness and rashes on applying skin products are your main complaint, you are S-dominant in SPA; if pigmentation and brown patches on your skin are your major worries, you are P-dominant; and if acne is your major concern, you are A-dominant. I will briefly go over your skin type and daily skincare for each of these types.

Remember, this is a book designed to help you care for your skin every day and not a medical book, so I am not discussing drug treatments but mostly natural and home skincare remedies and daily skincare cosmetic regimens for each type.

Let us now look at SPA classification of brown skin types:

S-TYPE (SENSITIVITY-PRONE SKIN)

Even if you don't think you have sensitive skin, it is sensible to try a new cosmetic or product that contains 'actives' by applying some behind your ears or on your arms. Remember the story of how I got a beetroot-red face from the silica and mineral content of the powdered rocks at Blue Lagoon?

How do we define sensitive skin? Essentially, it is the skin type that reacts easily to creams or products applied on the skin or to factors in the environment or diet.

Five keys to managing sensitive skin

1. Hydrate your body

Obviously, if the body is reacting to any toxins, the more hydrated your system is, the more dilute potential toxins are, so hydration is paramount. As the skin can only absorb a certain amount of moisture, it is important that people with sensitive skin drink plenty of water. If a person with sensitive skin drinks alcohol, the skin will be more prone to redness, so it is important to drink a glass of water for every glass of alcohol.

Hydrating your body may seem like common sense, but it is by no means universal. I know many dermatologists who believe that drinking water makes no difference to the skin. I believe it makes a huge difference. After all, as any medical student will tell you, one of the tests to determine if a child is dehydrated is to pinch the skin and assess the degree of dehydration.

'You are what you eat' is especially true of skin as it is the body's largest organ and naturally manifests externally any internal imbalances. Studies show that especially in middle-aged adults, there may be under-hydration leading to less microcirculation to the skin; so increasing the fluid intake increases subcutaneous tissue oxygen, improves wound healing and decreases skin infections.

2. Avoid soaps and use pH neutral products to cleanse the skin

As explained earlier, when pH is neutral, the liquid is neither acidic nor alkaline. The pH of human skin is 5.5, because the sebum (oil) in the lipid layer and sweat combine to lower the pH.

In the process of making soap, oil is mixed with an alkali, which means that soap is generally alkaline. Therefore, to make soap pH neutral or as close to water as possible, people usually add slightly acidic agents to neutralize it. In my cleansers, I use citrus extracts.

3. Bergamot is bad; oatmeal is awesome

I am mentioning this as I saw bergamot oils sold in cosmetic shops in India during my last visit there. Bergamot is a well-known psoralen (psoralens are a family of naturally occurring compounds used for conditions like psoriasis. They are found in the seeds of the plant *Psoralea corylifolia*, as well as in figs, celery and parsley. Psoralens like bergamot induce tanning and pigmentation. In fact, it was added to many sunscreens for this very effect as 'suntan lotions'. Tanning, you see, also has a protective effect from UV rays, which is why brown skin, with its easy tanning ability, has a low risk of UV damage and skin cancer. However, in brown and Asian skin types, we don't need any help with tanning as our skin tans beautifully anyway.

I remember a lady who consulted me with what I thought was a sun-induced skin reaction that had led to dark pigmentation on her cheeks. Initially, I investigated her diet and also arranged allergy tests. In the end, I realized she was reacting to the oil of bergamot in her sunscreen. Bergamot is a very useful extract. It belongs to the mint family and is used to flavour many products, including Earl Grey tea. Its extracts can induce uterine contractions in women and was used by ancient native Americans in medicines during labour. However, I have seen bergamot cause an irritant dermatitis that leads to hyperpigmentation on the skin.

Other than the risk of hyperpigmentation in brown skin, bergamot is also known to induce sweating, especially in hot conditions. The 'sweat lodges' of Native American medicine often used bergamot.

The term berlock dermatitis (in French *breloque* and in German *berlocke,* meaning pendant) has been given to the skin condition resulting from sun exposure following bergamot oil application. Especially in sunny conditions like in India, the use of bergamot could lead to the increased pigmentation that is a symptom of berlock dermatitis. Sometimes things we buy for a certain reason may indeed have the opposite effect. I have seen many Indian stores selling products containing bergamot, which are marketed as 'whitening'.

Even extracts of plants like ylang-ylang, tea tree and sandalwood can be a cause of irritant dermatitis. Sandalwood extracts are excellent as a bath oil on the body, but can cause an irritant dermatitis on the face. For anyone with sensitive skin, as discussed earlier, always test in the crook of an arm or behind the ear first.

> **Recipe for home-made oatmeal pack**
>
> One cup of rolled oats (not instant) mixed with a cup of mineral water and blended to create a consistent paste. Apply to skin and leave on as a mask for twenty minutes.

Oatmeal is often overlooked as a skin product. Of course, everyone knows the benefit of fibre in diet and the excellent low-glycaemic index of oatmeal as a food source. But oatmeal on skin? Colloidal oatmeal has been used since Roman and Greek times and oatmeal has properties that soothe skin and avoid irritation. It is often used as a bath scrub and moisturizer.

4. *Avoid these chemicals: parabens, formaldehyde donors, urea derivatives or isothiazolinones*

The use of parabens as preservatives in skin cosmetics, deodorants and shampoos has been as controversial as the reaction to the many studies published about them. They have also been shown to cause skin irritation in some people. In 2004, molecular biologist Dr Phillipa Darbre raised concerns when she reported in the UK that small concentrations of parabens (20 nanograms/gm) were found in breast cancers. There was an increasing realization that underarm deodorants containing parabens could have been the source. However, many subsequent studies exploring this link did not show any conclusive evidence that parabens caused cancer or that underarm deodorants posed any risk. The fact is, there are several alternative preservatives; parabens are only used as they are cheap and effective. I tell clients to avoid any product containing parabens as I have seen evidence of its skin-irritant effect. Other effects are still unknown, even if it is not a proved carcinogen.

Formaldehyde donors and urea derivatives have also been known to cause irritant dermatitis and are best avoided. However, in certain patients with hyperkeratotic conditions, i.e., where the skin is crusty and thick, we make up different kinds of urea-based creams. Isothiazolinones have been found in many types of glue and car products used by mechanics, and are a known source of contact dermatitis in motor mechanics. However, they can also be found in certain cosmetics, so look out for and avoid them. Needless to say, I do not use any of these preservatives.

Detecting harmful ingredients in cosmetics

- Parabens (look for ingredients that end in paraben, for example, butylparaben, methylparaben, ethylparaben, propylparaben, isobutylparaben); they could have harmful hormonal effects;
- Isothiazolinone (look for ingredients that end with this term, like methylchloroisothiazolinone); they are potential neurotoxins;
- Formaldehyde donors/urea derivatives: (look for variants of the words formaldehyde/DMDM hydantoin and urea or imidazolidinyl, like formalin, diazolidinyl urea, imidazolidinyl urea, DMDM hydantoin); they are potentially carcinogenic or can cause allergic and immune system problems.

---

5. Perfumes can be harmful

Perfumes cause amongst the most common irritant skin effects that dermatologists see. Some perfumes contain a very high alcohol content, which may be an irritant by itself, and cause a dermatitis leading to increased pigmentation when exposed to the sun. In India, many men who consulted me complained that they had developed increased cheek pigmentation from using aftershaves, especially those with high alcohol content. So if you want to have good skin and smell nice, spray the perfume on your clothing instead, or at least avoid the face. Even baby products contain fragrances (the 'baby smell') that cause skin irritation. I use natural and light citrus or lotus fragrances, and generally use essential oil-based natural perfumes. Our market research suggested that most people avoided completely

Key points

- Drink plenty of water. Hydration is good for skin. Oatmeal is a good hydrant for sensitive skin.

- Avoid soaps and use pH neutral cleansers as much as possible.

- Avoid bergamot, parabens, formaldehyde donors, urea derivatives or isothiazolinones in skincare products.

- Avoid strong perfumes and aftershaves. Use eau de cologne spray on your clothing rather than on naked skin.

unscented products. But we can and do produce – on request – some products that are free of all perfume.

Of course, as most skin doctors know, products advertised as 'unscented' may still contain skin allergens such as the ones discussed here.

P-TYPE (PIGMENTATION-PRONE SKIN)

Almost all the white-skinned patients I see are concerned about skin cancer, and virtually all my brown-skinned patients worry about skin pigmentation. When I talk about pigmentation, I mean hyperpigmentation, or dark patches. White patches or depigmentation, such as vitiligo/leucoderma are for discussion in medical literature and beyond the scope of a home skincare manual such as this. They cannot be managed by cosmetics alone.

Five keys to managing pigmentation of skin

1. Understand the cause of your pigmentation

Fundamentally, skin develops dark spots or patches because there is overproduction of melanin, the dark pigment of skin. In the chapter on skin anatomy (later in this book), there is a detailed discussion about melanocytes and their cellular anatomy.

Increased pigmentation or sunspots are caused because of overproduction of melanin, which is a protective effect, just as tanning is a protective mechanism. Freckling, such as in redheads, as far as I am concerned, is nothing but a pathetic attempt at tanning. Brown skin has large

Causes of skin hyperpigmentation
- Sun damage and sun exposure (dermatoheliosis)
- Inflammation or injury (post-inflammatory hyperpigmentation)
- Hormone imbalances or medications

melanosomes and therefore tans easily. However, when exposed to substances (remember the bergamot we just discussed?) that can stimulate more melanin, it may lead to patchy discolouration.

Because the cells are heavier and laden with pigment, brown skin is more prone to scarring. The darker the skin, greater the risk of thick scars. We only need to scratch ourselves and it leaves a mark for several months after the wound has healed. This is because the inflammation that results in response to the wound triggers higher melanin production. This inflammation is a normal response to injury and helps the cells to accumulate nutrients to facilitate healing of the wound. Unfortunately, it also leads to overproduction of melanin, causing post-inflammatory pigmentation.

Women are more prone to hyperpigmentation because hormonal changes caused by pregnancy or contraceptive pills can overstimulate melanocytes. This type of hyperpigmentation is called melasma. Over 50 per cent of women note some skin pigment changes during pregnancy. However, in most cases, this settles down on its own.

2. Avoid excessive sun exposure

This is perhaps most important for the pigmentation-prone skin type. It is best to avoid the sun between 11 a.m. and 4 p.m. (the highest UV radiation is usually from noon to 3 p.m., and I am allowing for an hour on either side). It is advisable to wear a hat or use an umbrella to shield the face if one has to go out in the sun. While many people advocate strong sunblocks >30, I recommend SPF 15 for brown skin. Many sunblocks contain elements that absorb UV rays that generate heat and could therefore stimulate tanning, especially in people with a propensity for hyperpigmentation. I've seen this effect on myself (I've explained this in more detail in the section on sun and sun protection). This is because most sunblocks originated as suntan lotions in Europe where people were trying to develop a tan that was considered healthy. Many sunscreens containing psoralens are now banned due to increased risk of skin cancer. However, some have bergamot or lavender oil too and those tend to stimulate pigmentation.

3. Look out for certain medications

Some commonly used medications can cause either photo-toxicity (an irritant reaction when exposed to the sun due to toxicity of chemicals) or photo-allergy (allergy like welts or urticaria on sun exposure).

Medications like retinoids used for severe acne can cause photosensitivity. Here is a list of the main medications used for other conditions that can cause skin photosensitivity or photo-allergy (make you more sensitive to sunlight or cause an allergic response when exposed to the sun):

- A: Antibiotics like tetracyclines (examples are doxycycline or minocycline used for acne or infections) or fluoroquinolones (common examples are ciprofloxacin or norfloxacin); anti-inflammatories like ibuprofen or naproxen or salicylates;
- B: Benzophenones and PABA (p-aminobenzoic acid, found in some sunscreens);
- C: Cardiac drugs like diatiazem or amiodarone; chlorpromazine (used in psychiatry);
- D: Diuretics like frusemide or hydrochlorthiazide (both used as anti-hypertensives; the former used in renal disease or to reduce fluid retention).

4. Avoid trauma to the face

Most post-inflammatory pigmentation is caused either due to trauma, surgery or the patient picking at pimples. Picking at acne or pimples even has a medical name – acne excoriée! It causes inflammation that stimulates melanin. Scratching at dermatitis or other itchy conditions can also lead to darkening of the skin.

Treat facial skin gently. In brown skin, it is important to be very cautious when opting for dermabrasion or laser treatments. Make sure you discuss with your skin doctor the risk of hyperpigmentation after any procedure.

The darker the skin, the more the risk of hyperpigmentation. This is the opposite of what people think – just as most westerners assume that brown skin doesn't tan.

Likewise, don't tweeze; it causes hair to break in the follicle, leading to inflammation. Old-fashioned Indian 'threading' is a little gentler on eyebrow or chin hair than tweezing, although that can also cause some irritation.

5. Melanin suppression

From a daily skincare point of view (which is the point of this book), I'd advise Vitamin C and natural fruit-based AHA peels (I had mentioned some home-made remedies earlier, which can be tried every fortnight or month, depending on sensitivity and response). Topical Vitamin C serums can also be effective for removing spots and these are available in many cosmetic brands. I have also developed a Vitamin C serum. If a person has significant hyperpigmentation that needs aggressive peels, lasers or drugs topically, I'd advise seeking medical help, because in brown skin there is a real risk of over-treatment which can lead to white patches that can only make matters worse.

A-TYPE (ACNE-PRONE SKIN)

As Figure 4 illustrates, the three main problems that lead to acne are excessive oil (sebum) production, blocked pores and inflammation/infection. So, for individuals with acne-prone

Key points

- Identify triggers: sun, inflammation or hormones.
- Avoid sun exposure and use sunscreen/hats.
- Avoid drugs and chemicals that are known to trigger pigmentation.
- Vitamin C serums in combination with oral Vitamin C are helpful.
- Mild facial peels with natural AHA extracts can help. For more aggressive peels or severe pigmentation, consult a cosmetic dermatologist.

skin, management of their skin essentially focuses on the points discussed earlier.

Five keys to managing acne-prone skin

1. Reducing oiliness of skin

Acne-prone skin has a genetic tendency to develop oiliness. This oil causes cells to stick to the bottom of the follicle. As we will see in the chapter on skin anatomy, epidermal cells migrate to the surface of the skin, but are stuck at the bottom of the follicles due to the sticky sebum (oil). As more oil builds up, the follicles dilate and the oil oozes out but oxidizes on the surface, causing brown skin to appear darker. This is why acne scars on brown skin appear darker than the rest of the skin.

Excessive oil on skin is best controlled by daily use of a gentle cleanser. As discussed earlier, a pH neutral cleanser is best. Salicylic acid is an FDA-approved topical acne treatment as it helps reduce the build up of cells within the follicle and also kills any bacteria within it.

To control oil on the skin, all that is needed is a good gentle daily cleanser.

2. Stopping pores from getting clogged

One of the fundamental principles of reducing oil blockage is using an exfoliator. This is because oil production is genetic and we cannot change our parents or grandparents. So while we cannot reduce oil production, we can manage this oil better, and prevent it from oozing onto skin and becoming oxidized. This is especially necessary in brown skin as it discolours more easily.

To prevent pores from getting clogged, exfoliate daily to stop the sebum from becoming hard. In most skin types, I would not advise exfoliation more than once a week, but in oily skin daily use of an exfoliant might be needed to control the oil. An exfoliator breaks up impacted cells and eases the blockage that leads to comedones (whiteheads and blackheads as shown in Figure 4).

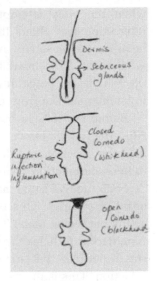

If someone with acne-prone skin uses an exfoliator daily, it prevents the comedones from recurring. In the Mikanis range, we have a gentle exfoliator with granules designed to unblock pores, and there are several other good exfoliators in the market. As daily exfoliation is advisable in oily acne-prone skin, I'd advise use of a gentle exfoliator, i.e., one that is not too abrasive.

Figure 4: Three main problems that lead to acne

3. Controlling the skin infection

All normal skin follicles (even in people who don't have acne) contain bacteria called propionibacterium acnes. This is part of the normal bacterial flora. However, this bacterium is anaerobic – it can only survive when starved of oxygen. In a normal hair follicle that is not clogged, it is found in the bottom of the hair follicle. Like rabbits, bacteria constantly reproduce and these propionibacterium acnes are no exception. However, as pores/follicles are normally open, the bacteria are also constantly being killed by oxygen from the atmosphere making its way down the open pore.

However, when a pore gets blocked, the oil builds up and hardens (or has not been exfoliated away), and oxygen cannot get down the shaft of the pore, causing an overpopulation of propionibacterium acnes bacteria, resulting in inflammation when the body attempts to fight the infection. Another interesting fact about these bacteria is that they actually break down the sebum and feed on the fatty acids produced as a result. This breakdown of the thicker sebum causes the follicles to bulge and eventually burst, leading to both inflammation of surrounding skin as well as scarring.

Before the follicle bursts, the pimples are white-tipped. After the follicle bursts, the body sends blood to the area to fight the infection and this is when the pimple turns red due to the accumulation of blood.

Sometimes, a facial massage or waxing can lead to sudden onset of pimples. This is because the massaging or waxing action may cause some inflammation of the hair follicle wall. As adjacent follicles swell, they crowd each other, creating small pockets that oxygen cannot flow into, leading to infection. This is the cause of pimples that appear overnight after waxing.

Most acne products contain some antibacterial ingredients to control infections caused by increased colonies of propionibacterium acnes. In an acne cleanser I've made for clients, we use salicylic acid. Some of the antibacterial ingredients you'll see in other acne medications include benzoyl peroxide and sulphur. Once the infection is too severe to control with topical antibacterials, the patient is often prescribed topical antibiotics (like clindamycin or erythromycin) or oral antibiotics (usually tetracyclines like minocycline or other antibiotics like erythromycin).

4. Avoid products that can worsen acne

As discussed earlier in this chapter, many ingredients found in cosmetics can actually clog pores and cause comedones to develop and worsen acne. It is important that people with acne look carefully at the ingredient list and avoid the main comedogenic ingredients.

The highly comedogenic ingredients that come to mind are cocoa butter, shea butter, olive oil and lanolin. Other ingredients known to be highly comedogenic are isopropyl myristate, butyl stearate, stearyl alcohol and oleic acid.

Most oils are comedogenic and moderately comedogenic ingredients include oils like coconut, sesame, peanut, mink, grapeseed or other ingredients like decyl oleate or myristyl lactate. Coconut oil is excellent for dry scalps, but best avoided on the face and forehead regions. However, the exception is clove oil, which is used in India for toothache – this has shown some antibacterial properties against propionibacterium acnes.

Likewise, while using hair gel or pomade or sprays, make sure you shield your forehead, as most hairstyling products are comedogenic, and allowing them to drift onto the forehead will cause occlusion of follicles and create small bump-like acne areas on the forehead.

5. *Look after your face by watching what you eat*

The importance of diet cannot be overemphasized. As I mentioned earlier, chocolates have been shown in studies to worsen acne, especially in young men. Late onset acne in women may be a sign of dairy intolerance. When my Canadian friend with acne gave up dairy products, she noted a marked improvement, so trial and error is a good idea if you suspect your problem might be dairy-related.

Are modern Asian diets more prone to acne? This was looked at in a large study in Korea which identified the following triggers: high-glycaemic foods (like sweets and sugary drinks, which is common amongst youngsters in India), high-iodine foods like nori seaweed/sushi and high dairy intake. Of course, eating sushi occasionally will not worsen acne, but on a daily basis it might. This study was the first to look at specific foods. The results are interesting for Indians as these foods are suspected culprits in India as well.

The following foods were found to be in the diet of acne-prone individuals and statistical analysis showed that their intake was significantly lower in the control group than in the acne group:

- Instant noodles
- Carbonated drinks
- Snacks like chips from packets, salted peanuts (or mixes similar to bhujia, etc.)
- Processed cheese
- Fried chicken
- Seaweed (nori as found in sushi)

Most youngsters with acne in India would be guilty of consuming the above foods.

Key points

- Cleanse face daily with a pH neutral acne skin cleanser.
- Exfoliate daily with a gentle facial exfoliator.
- Control skin infections and do not pick at pimples.
- Avoid comedogenic moisturizers and look carefully at ingredients in sunblocks.
- Most oils are bad for acne; clove oil has some antibacterial acne properties.
- Avoid carbonated drinks, processed fried food and processed snacks, instant noodles, fried chicken and seaweed; chocolates and dairy products can cause acne in young men and in women over twenty-five.

14

Circles v. Bags (Under Eyes)

I am getting dark circles around my eyes. Some days they look worse, but whatever I do they are noticeable. My friends say they are making me look tired; my parents say I am not sleeping enough. I am getting desperate, what should I do? ...

If I had to list the most common skin or cosmetic complaints that my brown-skinned patients bring to me, dark circles would be right on top. But to get a good understanding of dark circles around the eyes, we need to understand why it happens.

First of all, dark circles do not have a medical term for the simple reason that in most cases the reasons are physiological, not pathological, i.e., they are a normal bodily reaction and not a disease. So medical books don't have a fancy Latin name for the condition (although that did not stop doctors from trying to make it sound medical). Recently, Watanabe of Japan came up with a term called infra-orbital ring-shaped melanosis, which does not describe the condition adequately and hence has not found favour internationally. And yes, fatigue or tiredness does make them appear worse, so sleep is important for people susceptible to dark circles around eyes.

Bags around eyes causing puffiness in the mornings are also a nuisance, but less of a problem in brown skin (and more in white skin). Puffiness around the eyes can be caused due to the following: seasonal allergy (sinusitis, hay fever, etc.), salty diet (especially at night, causing fluid retention around the eyes) and crying (if you watched a tear-jerker of a movie at night, you may wake up with puffy eyes).

Dark circles around the eyes are different, even if there is an overlap in the causes of the two conditions. The four main causes for dark circles around the eyes are described below:

BAGGINESS OF EYELIDS

Bagginess of the skin under the eyes is a common cause of this appearance. In white-skinned people, this may simply appear as a bulgy lower eyelid, but in brown skin the contour change leads to darkened skin. When I trained in plastic surgery, I learnt that the underlying fat pads were no different in different skin types, so why the dark colour of baggy eyelids in brown skin? This is because the dermis of the skin becomes thicker due to the swelling, resulting in diffused reflection of light by the pigment found in brown skin, which in turn leads to darkening of the skin.

Therefore, the fundamental problem where someone has dark circles around the eyes and baggy eyelids is the thickened deeper layer of skin causing this effect. The treatment here is often surgical, because no cosmetic can really make a big difference. The only way to correct this is to fix the bulging lower eyelid.

A technique of fat-grafting developed by Dr Sydney Coleman of New York has shown great results in removing the ridge between bags and normal skin. Surgical excision of these fat pads may be done by a good plastic surgeon; CO_2 laser combined with a Q-switched laser has also shown good results in some studies.

However, some people have found this home-made recipe useful.

Recipe for home-made eyelid tightening cream

Rosemary twigs boiled and cooled to make an infusion. Egg whites and aloe vera gel mixed together. Add two tablespoons of the rosemary infusion with equal amount of the egg/aloe vera mixture. Some people like adding some Vitamin E oil as it acts as a natural preservative. An alternative is to mix the aloe vera gel with pureed cucumbers. Egg whites are supposed to have a tightening effect on the skin. So does the rosemary infusion.

PIGMENTATION (POST-INFLAMMATORY) UNDER THE EYELIDS CAUSED BY SKIN IRRITATION OR ALLERGY

If the dark circles are caused by skin allergy, it is important to find out the cause. Keeping a food diary for two weeks can help determine if certain foods, like dairy products, are causing the allergic reaction. Other allergens can include dust mites, animal fur, pollen and certain plants. If no specific allergen is found, it is important to avoid rubbing the eyes, because that will only make it worse. Consult your doctor and you may be prescribed anti-allergy eye drops or creams.

When testing for allergies, the most accurate method is a 'patch test', where a small amount of the suspected allergen is applied to the skin on the arm.

If it is not an allergy resulting from any food or plants, contact dermatitis could be a reason. I was travelling through Kerala and noticed hand-mixed pigments that Kathakali dancers were using around the eyes for theatrical effect. Before the show, we could see them using make-up and virtually all of them had post-inflammatory pigmentation around the eyelids.

Kajal or kohl is widely used in brown-skinned races to adorn the eyes or to ward off the 'evil eye'. In the Middle

East and Africa, many people grind the galena mineral into powder and use the lead sulphide to make up the kohl dye. This mineral contains lead sulphide, which constitutes the colour; however, this can also cause trachoma, a serious eye condition. In many states in the US, use of these products on children is prohibited. While kohl usually uses lead sulphide, Indian sindoor and surma contain lead oxide. If you are concerned that your kajal is causing eye irritation or dermatitis leading to dark circles, make sure you take it along when you are being tested for allergens.

The most important aspect of managing any dermatitis (whether allergic or irritant) is to moisturize. While discussing moisturizers, I had advised against the use of heavy moisturizers in brown skin as they could clog pores. The eyelid area is an exception as the skin is thinner and does not have hair follicles (except right at the margin of the eye). Hence, thicker moisturizers or even lip balms can be safely used as eye creams. However, please note that this is not recommended for people where irritants or allergy are not causing dermatitis and thereby circles around eyes. For normal skin, I prefer eye serums containing Vitamin C.

> **Recipe for home-made eye-moisturizing cream**
>
> In cases where irritants or allergy are a problem rather than bagginess of eyelids, blend two to four drops of rose hip and almond oil in either cocoa butter or beeswax. In any recipe using beeswax, this first needs to be heated to melt it and then allowed to cool before use.

EYELID OR PERI-ORBITAL SWELLING DUE TO RETENTION OF FLUID

Some people retain fluid around the lower eyelids just as some do around their legs or ankles. Gravity worsens the condition by making the fluid-filled skin sag as we become upright in the morning after sleeping at night. The eyelids look puffy in the mornings, and lack of sleep makes it even worse.

If you're prone to such swelling, it is important to reduce salt in the diet, especially salty processed snacks. Cranberry juice is a well-known plant diuretic and green tea has both antioxidant and diuretic effects.

BLOOD VESSELS LOCATED CLOSER TO SURFACE

This is fairly common in Indian skin types. The blood vessels under the eyelids are located closer to the skin surface leading to bluish darkening of skin of the lower eyelid. This is a genetic predisposition and is usually seen in mothers and daughters, both exhibiting the same dark colouration under eyelids.

Usually, if children have the problem (when parents don't), it is often due to atopic dermatitis from allergy (and the child is likely to outgrow it by adulthood), but if the daughter and mother have the problem, most likely it is due to this genetic predisposition. Very few remedies help here (although moisturizing with concealing moisturizers can help reduce the appearance). I make up a whitening day cream that can help conceal dark circles under eyelids; whitening in this context is used to denote reducing pigmentation as opposed to a 'fairness' cream – the latter I am philosophically opposed to.

As the person gets older, the fat on the face thins out, leading to dark circles becoming more prominent. It is also important to remember that when one wears spectacles, the eyes get lazy as they don't have to 'accommodate' to make images fall on the retina, and with time the eyes tend to get deeper-set, worsening this effect. So, in people prone to a genetic tendency to get dark circles, it is better to wear contact lenses or avoid spectacles.

Key points

- Dark circles around the eyes are a common complaint in Indian/brown-skinned individuals and a great source of distress.

- There are many causes, but in brown skin the causes can be divided into baggy eyelids, eyelid irritation or dermatitis, eyelid swelling due to fluid build-up, and the location of blood vessels closer to the skin due to an inherited tendency.

- When caused by eyelid bagginess, often surgical or laser options might be the best; home-made recipe: rosemary/egg white/aloe vera.

- When caused by irritation or allergy, moisturizing is the key (in addition to avoiding the cause); home-made recipe: beeswax/cocoa butter/almond/rose hip oil.

- When caused by fluid retention, avoid salty snacks; cranberry juice and green tea may be helpful as they are natural diuretics.

- When caused due to abnormally located blood vessels, concealing moisturizers are best; avoid wearing spectacles.

- General measures: avoid rubbing eyes, avoid dryness, moisturize every night and massage gently into eyelid skin, avoid spectacles if prone to dark circles under eyes.

15

Shaving v. Waxing

How can I avoid dark discolouration under my armpits?
They look bad when I wear sleeveless tops or blouses.
Also, what is the best method of hair removal in brown
skin? Is shaving better or waxing?
...

If dark circles under eyes are at the top on my list of complaints that my brown-skinned clients have, it is closely followed by discolouration or hyperpigmentation of underarm skin.

I'll first deal with the four main causes of dark discolouration of armpit or underarm skin and then talk briefly about hair removal.

INGREDIENTS IN UNDERARM DEODORANTS

Roll-on deodorants can worsen pigmentation of the armpits. In my experience (if the cause is the deodorant), it is usually because of the perfume in the deodorant or the alcohol content. As we discussed earlier, perfumes and eau de cologne have been known to stimulate pigmentation in brown skin while alcohol content causes irritation and also dehydrates the skin, thereby aggravating the increased pigmentation.

I would, therefore, recommend using unscented deodorants for the armpits.

SHAVING OR WAXING ARMPIT HAIR

I made an interesting discovery when I looked at an area of pigmentation using a skin scanner to assess the damage. When you shave, you cut across the surface of the hair, which means that there are residual hairs in the follicles that grow out (the rate of growth depends on the individual). As the hair in the follicle is dark, it tends to give the skin a darker appearance.

I first realized this when I saw an older patient who complained that after years of getting dark discolouration of armpits, he was getting white discolouration. All that had happened was that his hair had turned grey.

If you have just begun to shave and you notice a discolouration, switch to waxing, which removes the hair more cleanly. You will surely notice a difference.

MEDICAL DISEASES SUCH AS ACANTHOSIS NIGRICANS

When people look up acanthosis nigricans in Internet search engines, they tend to panic as it is often linked to an underlying cancer. But the condition is very rare in brown skin types. In people with brown skin, acanthosis nigricans is usually benign – not dangerous, only of cosmetic concern.

Essentially, this is a condition that causes hyperpigmentation and thickening (hyper-keratosis) of armpits and neck skin, usually in overweight individuals. It is more common among adults, although sometimes it is seen in overweight adolescents. One way to differentiate this from the pigmentation caused due to irritation from shaving is that this usually involves skin of folds like armpits and neck. In India, I have seen it occurring more in south India, where the Dravidian skin type is darker.

Certain hormones can worsen this condition. An overproduction of insulin as well as polycystic ovarian syndrome, where the levels of luteinizing hormones (which stimulate ovulation) and follicle-stimulating hormones are usually elevated, are both causes of acanthosis nigricans. Overproduction of insulin may simply be because your diet is too rich in refined sugars and sweets. Or it could be hormonal and related to other hormonal disorders. Overweight people with hyperpigmentation of neck and armpits are at high risk of developing non-insulin-dependent diabetes. Watching what you eat is very important.

Both acanthosis nigricans and polycystic ovarian syndrome are associated with obesity. Less your weight, the less likely it is that you have the condition. If you suspect that you suffer from acanthosis nigricans, consult your doctor. In polycystic ovarian syndrome, the weight gain is also often associated with increased hair production on the face. Sometimes, hormonal medication or sugar-lowering medications like metformin are used.

EXCESSIVE CELL PRODUCTION

As discussed earlier, cells from deeper layers of skin migrate upwards and form keratinocytes. An excessive production of these cells can lead to hyper-keratosis, which may be harmless or may be due to an underlying cause (rarely, cancers could be the cause too). If you have dark discolouration in your armpits, use some sticky tape and strip it away. If some of the discolouration comes off on the tape, it is because of overproduction and excessive build-up of cells.

In this situation, the treatment is scrubbing and exfoliation to prevent the cells that build up from accumulating and causing hyperpigmentation.

Vitamin C is excellent to reduce pigmentation and oral supplementation is needed in addition to creams (so eat oranges or sweet limes daily). Again, as with bags under the eyes, I sometimes make up whitening creams to reduce pigmentation which help mask dark colour of the armpits.

Irrespective of the cause of underarm pigmentation or darkening, the treatment is aimed at lessening the cosmetic problem. Many doctor-prescribed bleaching treatments have

> **A south Indian grandmother's recipe to treat armpit pigmentation**
>
> Lemon juice (Vitamin C helps reduce pigmentation), turmeric (antibacterial and anti-fungal effects, which can help reduce odour under armpits) and sandalwood oil drops. Mix lemon juice and turmeric with sandalwood oil and apply under armpits and leave overnight. The sandalwood works as a perfume.

been tried, and the most successful in Asian skin types have been a combination of retinoic acids and lactic acid gels. Some have advocated adding hydroquinone as well, but like I said earlier, I tend to avoid it. You can consult your doctor regarding the use of retinoic acids and lactic acid to help reduce discolouration by using ointments. Of course, if there is a cause, either metabolic or hormonal, that will need addressing. Make sure you have a sugar test to rule out diabetes, especially if you are overweight. Sometimes lasers can be tried as a last-ditch attempt.

Now, regarding hair removal for underarms, the following is a home-made 'hair-removal wax' recipe that a patient from Brazil told me about, when I was talking to her about this book dedicated to brown skin. Because she lives in New Zealand, she is also partial to manuka honey due to its healing properties. (Needless to say, I didn't ask her if this was good for the famed 'Brazilian' wax.)

Recipe for home-made hair-removal wax

Lemon juice – two tablespoons, honey or aloe vera – two tablespoons, brown sugar – two cups, water – half a cup. Heat these ingredients in a microwave or saucepan to 120°C and pour into a bottle to store. To use, heat for twenty seconds or so in a microwave to make molten and warm. Microwave times may vary. Test to make sure it is not too hot or you will burn yourself. Do not allow children near you.

You can apply it with a flat stick, spatula or a doctor's tongue-depressor onto the hair-bearing area. Place cotton strips (cutting up an old white cloth into reusable white cotton strips will do) immediately after applying this 'wax' and pull against direction of hair growth..

Key points

Hair Removal

- If you are prone to hair follicles making armpits look dark, wax instead of shaving.

- If your skin is very oily, use a foaming shave gel; if not, gel will do.

- After shaving, moisturize well and leave overnight; it is best to shave at night after a bath to soften hair follicles first and then moisturize the underarm region with a heavy cold-cream-like moisturizer.

- Home-made hair removal wax: brown sugar/honey/lemon.

Discolouration/Pigmentation

- If shaving makes your armpits look dark due to residual hair follicles, wax.

- If overweight, consult a doctor to check your sugar and rule out conditions like acanthosis nigricans or other hormonal problems.

- Avoid perfumed deodorants and exfoliate armpits if you are getting build-up of skin cells.

- Home-made armpit cream: lemon/turmeric/sandalwood.

16

Vitamins B v. C v. D

You say that Vitamin C is good for skin. Can you elaborate? And is there any other vitamin that I should know about in this context?

...

No discussion about sun and skin is complete without an understanding of the role of vitamins D and C. These two are the most important with respect to skin. However, it is worth looking at Vitamin B more closely, as 'B complex' tablets are possibly the most widely taken supplements.

VITAMIN B

Vitamin B consists of the following vitamins (folic acid or folate also technically belongs to this group):

- B1 (thiamine)
- B2 (riboflavin)
- B3 (niacin)
- B5 (pantothenic acid)
- B6 (pyridoxine)
- B7 (biotin)
- B12 (cobalamin)

Of all the B vitamins, the one with specific action on skin is B3 or niacin. This is converted into niacinamide in the body, especially when intake exceeds the amount that is required. Niacin is found in yeast (Marmite or Vegemite contain yeast), eggs, fish (especially salmon), green beans and lentils. A century ago, deficiency of niacin commonly caused pellagra (symptoms include diarrhoea and dementia), but it is rare these days. Vitamin B3 is used to treat high cholesterol and certain skin conditions. But more recently research has focused on niacin as a 'beauty vitamin'.

We now know that niacinamide when topically applied to skin reduces yellowing, wrinkling, red blotchiness and pigmentation in ageing facial skin. It also stimulates collagen synthesis. Niacinamide may have particular benefits in Asian and brown skin as our skin type is prone to pigmentation as we have discussed several times. Further tests done in Japan showed that a 2 per cent solution also reduced sebum (oil) production – and so may be of benefit to those with excessively oily skin.

Vitamin D

Vitamin D is produced when the epidermis of the skin is exposed to the sun. It is necessary for calcium formation in the body, which means that adequate levels of Vitamin D are needed for healthy bones and teeth. In India, because traditionally people want to avoid tanning, they stay out of the sun as much as possible. In Australia and New Zealand, due to the high risk of skin cancer, sunscreens are the commonest form of skincare products used. There was also a growing concern whether the use of sunscreen reduces Vitamin D. Fortunately, this has now been shown to be a myth: using sunscreen does not do that. The factors that really determine optimal Vitamin D absorption is the time of sun exposure and the amount of body surface exposed.

While Vitamin D is mostly produced by the skin from sun exposure, fish oils (especially oily fish like salmon and cod) contain large amounts of it; eggs and dairy products contain smaller amounts of Vitamin D. However, because many Indians are vegetarians who do not eat eggs or fish, and also avoid sun exposure, there is an epidemic of Vitamin D deficiency – especially as dark skin inherently absorbs less Vitamin D than white skin. In older people, such a lack of Vitamin D could lead to softer bones (osteomalacia). In adults, it can not only lead to brittle bones and teeth, but also affect general health. In young children, it might mean severe bone deformities like rickets. While breastfeeding is good for the baby, if the mother is Vitamin D deficient, it leads to the baby becoming deficient as well, and could lead to serious problems. When the baby is not exclusively breastfed, many infant formulae are fortified with Vitamin D.

In my skin clinics, I have noted that almost all my brown-skinned patients seem to lack adequate Vitamin D levels. Some studies have been conducted in the UK on Indian subcontinental patients, which suggest that perhaps diet may also be a factor: the unleavened flour of chapattis tends to bind calcium further, aggravating the problem of calcium metabolism caused by Vitamin D deficiency.

In my brown-skinned patients, I advise short bursts of sun exposure. The skin can only absorb a limited amount of Vitamin D, and spending all day in the sun does not necessarily lead to much higher Vitamin D levels than spending half an hour in the sun twice a day.

Traditionally, UVB has been considered a major source of Vitamin D, but most clinical studies used latitude or time as proxies for actual measurement of the UV dose on skin. In 2011, Morten Bogh of Malmo University Hospital in Sweden undertook an experiment measuring various UV doses with skin exposure. His findings were interesting: significant UVB responses correlated with 6 per cent and 12 per cent exposure of body surface but saturated at 24 per cent of body-surface exposure. Therefore, if you wanted to absorb enough Vitamin D, you would have to expose enough skin. (For example, wearing a T-shirt and shorts would give you enough exposure as each arm equates to 9 per cent of body-surface area and each leg 18 per cent. That said, as legs and arms are circumferential, it is impossible to get all parts of an arm or leg exposed to the sun at the same time.)

Interestingly enough, the natural response of brown skin to the sun actually increases the risk of Vitamin D deficiency. Brown skin responds to sun exposure by tanning – a protective mechanism as also an immune response. We have discussed earlier that the brown skin type has a large melanosome in the cell that causes the skin to darken. This large melanosome positions itself directly above the nucleus and acts as a 'shade' for the nucleus of the cell, which is where all the genetic material is stored. While this protects brown skin types from genetic damage to the skin, which prevents us from getting skin cancers, this 'shading' also reduces penetration of UVB rays and therefore results in less production of Vitamin D.

For a long time it was believed that calcium was most important for bone development and women were advised to take calcium supplements. However, in clinical studies conducted on 72,000 nurses by Professor Walter Willett at Harvard Medical School, it was shown that women with the highest intakes of Vitamin D (from food or supplements) had a 37 per cent lower risk of hip fracture than did the lowest consumers of Vitamin D. This study inferred that a high Vitamin D intake was more important than high calcium intake for prevention of hip fractures.

While the Harvard study on nurses was conducted on subjects with mostly white skin, it is even more important for brown-skinned people to take Vitamin D supplements (given all the reasons we've discussed above).

Vitamin D deficiency leads to calcium deficiency and this has major effects on health, especially in the brown skin type. When we have low calcium levels, our bodies increase levels of two hormones – parathormone and calcitriol – which result in absorption of calcium from the intestines. This leads to more calcium inside our cells (intra-cellular calcium); high intra-cellular calcium levels lead to higher blood pressure and cellular fat. This finding that low dietary calcium raises intra-cellular calcium has been called the 'calcium paradox', and there is a possibility that it may also play a part in the development of arteriosclerosis, Alzheimer's, diabetes and muscular dystrophy. With a high vegetarian population and dark skin that avoids sunlight, India is now seeing an increase in heart as well as arterial disease, even among people who are maintaining otherwise healthy diets. People in India are often advised to take calcium supplements. I have many visiting clients from India who routinely consume calcium tablets. But taking calcium without correcting Vitamin D levels worsens heart disease; this may also be contributing to rising levels of heart disease in India.

I recommend 1.25mg of Vitamin D (in the form of Vitamin D3 50,000 I.U. or chole-calciferol) once a month for most of my patients. However, please check with your doctor if this regimen is suitable for you as taking too much Vitamin D can lead to increased calcium levels, which in turn can lead to kidney stones or heart irregularities. As with anything, too much of a good thing can be harmful.

It is important to note that while the pigment in our skin reduces sun damage, ultraviolet damage to the eyes is a major factor in the formation of cataracts in brown skin types. In India, in general, sunglasses are used less than in Western countries. According to WHO, 20 per cent of cataracts in India are caused by the sun.

A study published in the *American Journal of Clinical Nutrition* in 2000 clearly showed that obesity decreased the

Key points

- Vitamin D is produced by the skin on sun exposure.

- Vitamin D is necessary for healthy teeth, bones and general health.

- Brown-skinned individuals are more prone to Vitamin D deficiency as they generally avoid sun; dietary and genetic factors and tanning also contribute to the deficiency.

- Short bursts of sun exposure, about thirty minutes twice a day, are enough as there is a limit to the skin's capacity to produce Vitamin D in a day.

- Monthly supplementation with Vitamin D is advisable in people with brown skin type.

- Low Vitamin D levels can lead to high blood pressure, arterial disease and muscular diseases.

- Obesity reduces the availability of Vitamin D in the body.

bioavailability of Vitamin D, i.e., the fatter the individual, the less Vitamin D they were able to utilize. Therefore, maintaining a healthy lifestyle with plenty of exercise helps.

We've now established that Vitamin D is produced by the skin and improves general well-being. But does it have any specific skin benefits? The answer is yes. It is involved with the process of keratinocyte formation, which we discussed earlier. So, Vitamin D reduces excessive dryness and crusting of skin. In conditions like psoriasis, which cause excessive proliferation of skin cells, or in skin conditions that involve pigmentation changes, Vitamin D analogues like Calcipotriol are used in treatment. Calcipotriol has also been shown to improve skin immunity and protect against microbial infections of the skin. Further, it has also been shown to reduce damage to skin after UV and ionizing radiation.

Vitamin C

Vitamin C has two primary functions with respect to skin: firstly, it is important for collagen synthesis; secondly, it helps in healing wounds. As we discussed in the chapter on skin anatomy, collagen is essential to maintain skin architecture and for younger-looking skin.

It is incredible how much wisdom is present in ancient Indian remedies. When I was growing up, I used to observe villagers in the fields rub orange peels on their arms before going out in the sun. Meena, a good friend of mine who is a radiologist and divides her time between India and the US, remembers her mother asking her to rub oranges on her skin during her childhood.

So what is special about oranges? Vitamin C and more Vitamin C! We may have developed unique Vitamin C extracts for use in cosmetics, but, essentially, citrus fruits have an abundance of Vitamin C.

Because Vitamin C is a good antioxidant, it helps reduce

skin damage and the wrinkle formation it causes. However, there is a problem with Vitamin C delivery. This is because the skin is essentially a barrier designed to keep things out of our body. Hence, only a small amount of Vitamin C is absorbed through the skin. This is where concentration and composition of Vitamin C extracts is important. It is, therefore, also important to take Vitamin C orally every day. I generally advise 100 mg which is equivalent to two orange slices daily; an orange a day would be even better for the skin and provide you with more than your daily Vitamin C needs. Bee, a former student of mine, who works as a dermatologist in Thailand herself, takes 1,000 mg Vitamin C daily, as do many dermatologists I know. Like I said earlier, though, when taken in pill form, Vitamin C has little effect on skin (even if it may help other organs).

The late Dr Linus Pauling, twice Nobel laureate and champion of Vitamin C science, used to take mega doses of Vitamin C, greater than 1,000 mg per day. Pauling, at the age of ninety-two, was still sprightly, and in 1993 spoke about his theories linking Vitamin C disease and heart disease. Many creatures that can repair their tissues (like lizards replacing their injured or lost tails) have been shown to produce Vitamin C in their bodies to help skin healing. Pauling said that one of the great misfortunes of evolution was when ancient man embarked on a diet rich in fruits containing Vitamin C, leading to the body losing its natural ability to synthesize Vitamin C. This left today's primates (including humans) as one of the few groups of animals that must get the vitamin through diet alone. Pauling not only wrote extensively on the benefits of Vitamin C in fighting the common cold virus, but also on Vitamin C reducing risks of heart disease by reducing levels of lipoprotein-A, which causes the build-up of plaques in blood vessels. Unlike human beings, animals that manufacture their Vitamin C and have much higher levels of the vitamin in their bodies, have very little lipoprotein-A in their blood and thereby do not get heart disease. As I always say, natural sources are better than pills and I will discuss this later. An orange a day may indeed keep the skin doctor away!

While citrus fruits like oranges have the highest concentrations, Vitamin C is also found in the following fruits and vegetables: broccoli, blueberries, cranberries, cabbage, cauliflower, mango, papaya and strawberries.

Key points

- Vitamin C is critical for collagen synthesis and younger-looking skin.

- An orange a day gives you more than the Vitamin C your skin needs.

- As Vitamin C is not absorbed via the skin easily, it is important to also take Vitamin C orally daily.

- Vitamin C has also been shown to have benefits in reducing plaques that can lead to heart disease.

17

UVA v. UVB

When I read about sunblocks I am confused about UVA and UVB and the chemicals in sunscreens. I know you've said that in brown skin we only need SPF 10–15. Can you explain the ingredients of sunblocks and the differences between them?

...

To begin with, let's look at how sunblocks or sunscreens work. They either absorb and neutralize UV rays, or work as reflectors for UV rays.

In absorbing UV rays, the sunscreen generates heat and this is why sometimes in brown skin they may stimulate tanning (the opposite of what most Indian or Asian people are trying to do, which is why I do not recommend higher SPF for brown skin). Absorbent sunscreens can also worsen redness in people with sensitive skin (which is why I personally go for the lowest sunscreen needed in Indian skin conditions).

Titanium oxide and zinc oxide are reflectors of UV rays. Titanium oxide is more often used, because zinc oxide gives that white painted look as you often see around cricketers' lips – remember Andrew Symonds who played for Australia? If you have sensitive skin or skin that darkens easily, make sure your sunscreen contains zinc or titanium oxide.

The second issue to discuss is blocking UVA and UVB rays. One simple way to remember the difference between the two is that UVB causes burning of skin and UVA causes ageing. UVB does not penetrate car windows or transparent clothing, but UVA can. UVB generally cannot penetrate dermis of skin, but UVA can.

ABC OF UV RADIATION

Ultraviolet A = ageing (causes wrinkling of skin and implicated in melanoma skin cancers in white skin; penetrates dermis of skin).

Ultraviolet B = burning (causes sunburn and tanning in brown skin types; penetrates epidermis of skin).

Ultraviolet C = cataracts (fortunately most UVC is filtered out by the atmosphere, but looking directly at the sun is harmful).

Figure 5 helps us understand the size of UV radiation when compared to other forms of environmental radiation.

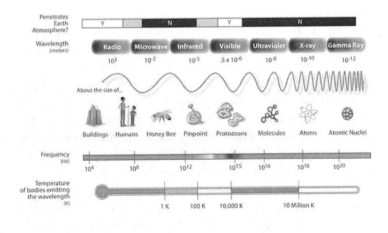

Figure 5: Electromagnetic spectrum

It is important to remember that the immune system in children is not fully developed and tanning in brown skin is a defence mechanism – which is why brown-skinned people have a very low risk of skin cancer when compared to white skin. So if we use sunblocks or sunscreens in dark children under the age of three, especially in those with brown or Asian skin (with an inherent ability to tan), we run the risk of increasing their chances of skin cancer later on (as the body's immune system does not 'learn' to tan properly). My advice, therefore, is to use caps and hats rather than sunscreen on children under age three.

A 'broad-spectrum' sunscreen is one that filters out both UVA and UVB rays. One other aspect is that the rise in SPF only minimally changes the strength of the filter. I had said earlier that I recommend only a low SPF of 15 to 30 for brown skin. This is because an SPF 30 sunscreen filters out only 4 per cent more UV when compared to one with SPF 15. Increasing the SPF does not give you an incrementally higher UV filtering effect.

For my brown skin clients, I make up a sunscreen with SPF 15 to 30 containing zinc or titanium oxide – the former I use for more natural formulations. However, we need to be careful of a few ingredients. Some people may be allergic to a specific ingredient. For instance, PABA was widely used because of its effectiveness against UVB, but many people developed allergies to it. These days, few manufacturers still use this ingredient. I'd definitely avoid PABA-containing sunblocks. The other issue to note is that many manufacturers use antioxidants, i.e., either botanicals and vitamins in sunscreens to help scavenge free radicals. But some botanicals, like bergamot, are well known to cause pigmentation in brown skin. From a pure sun protection point of view, these afford no benefit (although they may help repair UV damage later); so I'd definitely avoid sunscreens containing bergamot.

List of FDA-approved organic sunscreens

UVA
- Avobenzone (Parsol 1789, butyl methoxydibenzoylmethane)
- Methyl anthralinate (Ensulizole, Meradimate)
- Dioxybenzone (benzophenone-8)
- Oxybenzone (benzophenone-3, Eusolex 4360, Uvinul M-40)
- Sulisobenzone (benzophenone-4)
- Mexoryl SX (Ecamsule, terephthalylidene dicamphor sulfonic acid)

UVB
- p-aminobenzoic acid (PABA)
- Octyl dimethyl p-aminobenzoic acid (padimate O)
- Homosalate (homomenthyl salicylate)
- Octyl salicylate (octisalate)
- Trolamine salicylate
- Cinoxate (ethoxy ethyl-p-methoxycinnamate, Neo Heliopan E1000, Uvinul N-539)
- Octinoxate (octyl methoxycinnamate, Parsol MCX, Escalol 557, Eusolex 2292)
- Octocrylene (2-ethylhexyl-2-cyano-3, 3-diphenylacrylate)
- Ensulizole (phenylbenzimidazole sulfonic acid)

Inorganic Sunscreens
UVA/UVB (broad spectrum)
- Titanium dioxide
- Zinc oxide

Key points

- UV radiation is harmful to skin (UVB = burns skin; UVA = ages skin).

- Sunscreens are useful to prevent damage from UV rays.

- Sunscreens can absorb/neutralize or reflect UV rays. Absorbent sunscreens can worsen sensitive skin or stimulate tanning in brown skin.

- In brown skin, an SPF of 15 should suffice.

- Avoid sunscreen in children under three as it could potentially increase the risk of skin cancer.

- Avoid sunscreens with PABA (p-aminobenzoic acid) or those containing bergamot.

18

Hair v. Bare

My hair seems to be falling out in clumps. Sometimes it seems OK. Does hair-shedding have seasonal variations? I am from south India and whatever I try, my hair tends to get curly. Any solutions?

...

Let's begin by looking at the general characteristics of hair, specifically dark hair. As discussed earlier, most dark hair follicles are similar to hair follicles in Caucasian skin. However, in the southern states of India, especially Kerala and parts of Tamil Nadu bordering Kerala, hair follicles are curved, resulting in hair with short curls.

Black hair is thick and therefore the hair follicles are denser (which is why Asian hair, more than any other hair type is exported to make wigs). If the hair is very thick there will be a higher number of sebaceous glands in it; this is why dark hair is prone to oiliness.

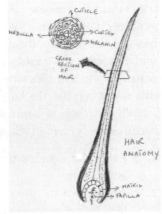

Figure 6: Anatomy of a hair follicle

A large bulb-like structure, called the papilla (see Figure 6), forms the base of the hair follicle. This is made up mostly of connective tissue. Unlike skin cells, cells in the papilla rarely divide. It is surrounded by a matrix made up of epithelial cells that produce pigment, i.e., melanocytes, as we discussed earlier when studying skin anatomy. Cell division here is responsible for development of hair fibre and root sheaths. The matrix is made up of fast-developing cells. When a patient undergoes chemotherapy, the drugs usually target fast-developing cells, including the matrix (because tumour cells too are fast developing). This is why chemotherapy leads to hair loss. Because the matrix surrounds the papilla and is first exposed to toxins, it is important to avoid chemicals from coming into contact with the scalp.

Now, to address your question about hair cycles. Even though some people have scalp hair extending to their waistlines, every individual has a 'hair cycle limit', which is the point at which 90 per cent of the hair has reached maximal length. In scalp hair, this is on average three to four years (of course, there are individual variations as in anything). This is true even for eyebrow hair. On an average, the cycle limit for eyebrow hair is four to six months. This means that scalp hair has a much longer 'limit' when compared to eyebrow hair, which is why you couldn't grow your eyebrows down to your waist. If you see older people with really bushy eyebrows, this is not because the hair is longer, but because it is denser.

Why is there a limit on the hair cycle length? This is because hair grows in stages:

1. Follicular development stage (in which the hair follicle is formed);
2. Anagen, or the growth phase of hair; on average, three to four years for scalp hair and four to six months for eyebrow hair;

Key points

- Asian hair has the fastest growth rate, followed by Caucasian hair. African hair has the slowest growth rate.

- Hair follicles look similar in Indian/Latino and Caucasian skin; African hair arises from a curved hair follicle. This curved hair-follicle appearance is also seen in south India, especially around Kerala.

- White skin has less hair growth overall and is prone to dryness; brown skin has greater hair growth and is prone to oiliness.

- While male-pattern baldness is genetic, causes of hair loss can include iron and thyroid deficiencies.

3. Catagen, or the regressing phase of hair (this is when hair regresses or involutes – no connection to receding hair as we are discussing individual hair follicles here, not hair patterns); on average two to three weeks;

4. Telogen, or the resting phase of hair; on average two to three months for scalp hair and around nine months for eyebrow hair. Fortunately, eyebrow hair has a long resting period and, therefore, one does not need regular eyebrow trims;

5. Exogen, or shedding phase (this happens when several hairs arise from one hair follicle, i.e., 'twinning' hairs, and some of these are discarded.

When the telogen phase is more prominent, there are not enough cells growing and this leads to baldness. This is why in India, where iron deficiency is common due to vegetarian diets, it is important to check iron levels if someone is losing hair suddenly. Iron and thyroid deficiencies are among the causes of hair loss.

While we are on the topic of hair follicles, a common complaint I am faced with is to do with ingrown hair. What causes ingrowing? Is one type of hair removal method less likely to cause ingrowing?

Shaving can cause ingrown hairs. As we discussed, the darker one's skin, the more curly the hair follicles are. Further, especially in southern India, curly hair is common.

All razors cut hair at an angle and when the hair is curled right around, the tips can pierce through skin to cause ingrown hair. How does one avoid ingrown hair? For a start, make sure your razor is sharp. Next, it is best to shave after a warm shower or bath so the hair is soft. Shaving in the direction of hair growth reduces the risk of ingrowing, but will not give you as close a shave as shaving against hair growth. A dry shave, i.e., using an electric razor, reduces the risk of ingrowing, but the shave will be less 'close'. If you prefer a wet shave, 'buffing'

Key points

HAIR FOLLICLE HEALTH

- Stress and smoking can cause hair loss.
- When using a hair dryer, avoid setting it too hot.
- When using hair products, avoid those containing alcohol.
- When using hair products like gel or mousse, apply to hair but not to scalp.
- Wet your hair before entering a pool, so hair soaks up water rather than chlorinated water.
- Whenever possible, use a cap to protect your hair in chlorinated pools.

the area to be shaved with a wet cloth reduces the curling and, therefore, reduces the risk of ingrown hair. A multi-blade razor always gives you a closer shave than a single-blade one. It is preferable to have a razor that contains a moisture-strip.

Does shaving or waxing worsen ingrowing? Most definitely, waxing is better if you want to avoid ingrown hairs. Women especially prefer waxing along the bikini line for this very reason. Further, over a period of time, waxing damages the hair follicle and this leads to less hair growth.

What about threading? Threading is an Indian technique where a twisted thread is used to pull out hairs. Typically, the 'threader' holds one end of the thread between their teeth and the other is wrapped around one of the fingers. Given these technical considerations, it is not used for private parts. Threading is most commonly used for eyebrow hair removal, for which it is the best solution. It causes no ingrowing, because it pulls the hair out clean, and doesn't affect the skin as much as waxing does. In people with white skin, excessive waxing could increase wrinkling.

Waxing must be avoided if one is on retinoids or AHA (we have discussed these earlier) as these make skin more sensitive and can cause it to peel. In general, you need to stop using these products a fortnight before waxing.

People seeking more permanent hair removal often combine threading with laser treatment. But it is best to wait for a month after threading before commencing laser treatment.

Hair removal creams can be skin irritants, given that they have to contain chemicals. They are best avoided, but if you want to use them, first apply a 'test patch' to make sure it does not irritate your skin.

Key points

HAIR REMOVAL

- Waxing causes less ingrown hair when compared to shaving.

- Shaving after a warm bath and buffing the area with a soft cloth reduces the risk of ingrowing.

- Threading works well; if you are planning laser treatment, wait a month after the last threading.

- Waxing works well and does not cause ingrown hair; however, avoid waxing when on retinoids or AHA.

- Laser hair removal actually works better on dark hair due to the presence of melanin pigment. But dark skin is more prone to scarring and increased pigmentation.

19

Sweat v. Oil

I don't moisturize routinely as I sweat and think moisturizers will make it worse. However, I note my skin tends to peel and this gets worse after a swim. Any advice? Further, my boyfriend says men don't need moisturizing. Is this true?

...

Skin is an organ, like the liver or lung – it is the largest organ in the body. It accounts for about 16 per cent of human body weight. The outer layer, the epidermis, makes up 5 per cent of skin and the dermis, the deeper layer, makes up 95 per cent of it. The epidermis produces Vitamin D on exposure to sunlight, but it is essentially 'dead' – that is, it has no blood vessels. The outer layer derives nutrition from the underlying dermis, via the basement membrane that separates the two layers.

Our skin colour is made brown by the distribution of melanocytes, which are found in the basal layer of the epidermis and also in the matrix of the hair bulbs. Cells in the epidermis generally have origins in the basal layer; as they divide, the cells migrate upwards. As this movement takes place, they are filled with a dry protein called keratin and the cells are then called keratinocytes. Keratin is what makes up both hair and nails. Basically, this process is like sun drying a mango. As it dries, the mango pulp becomes dehydrated, thicker and harder. During the keratin-forming stage, a lipid complex too forms and spreads between cells to form a barrier layer, creating a line of protection for the skin and preventing loss of moisture. The process is a bit like using putty or mortar to fill up the gaps between bricks.

Skin with a poor lipid barrier is like a wall that has gaps between bricks. Such skin will be unhealthy and prone to breakdown, just like unstable bricks. Cold weather or very hot dry weather can both damage the lipid layer and dehydrate skin. That is what you are describing when the weather is hot. Using soap also strips the skin of natural oils that make up this lipid layer, dehydrating it. Conditions like dermatitis and dandruff are inherently caused by loss of skin moisture, because of which the skin becomes dry and flaky.

If your skin has lost its lipid layer or is not moisturized, wrinkles and frown lines become more noticeable, making you look older. This is why moisturizing is extremely important. Many owners of beauty salons in India I spoke to worried that moisturizing made people sweat more. This is a myth because if you use the right type of moisturizer, you will not sweat. Moisturizing is extremely important for younger-looking skin and the best time to moisturize is after a bath or a shower. If you use a moisturizer that is too heavy for humid Indian conditions, like shea or cocoa butter, it can make you sweat. So, use a light moisturizer or one with a skin-barrier protectant like silicone, which will not make you sweat and will replenish the lipid layer. We have discussed making your own moisturizer earlier.

The dermis is the deeper layer of skin. This layer is responsible for maintaining the shape of the skin as it contains collagen fibres, as also sweat glands, oil glands, hair follicles and blood vessels.

Key points

LIPID-LAYER DAMAGE

- Flaky skin or 'tiling' of skin can indicate dehydration.
- Skin that feels tighter after a bath.
- Itchy skin, especially in winter.
- Stinging of skin in summer, especially when sweaty.

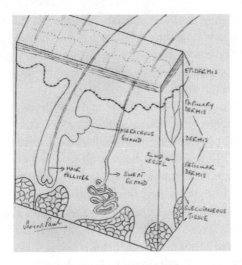

Figure 7: Skin anatomy diagram

The dermis contains fibroblast cells that produce collagen. Thin collagen bundles are located in its upper layer called the papillary dermis and thick parallel bundles of collagen in its deeper layer called the reticular dermis (see Figure 7).

There are two types of fibres produced by the fibroblasts of the dermis. Collagen is responsible for firmness and plumpness of skin and a loss of collagen can make the skin appear loose and wrinkled. Elastin affects elasticity, i.e., the ability of skin to return to its shape when pinched. In brown skin, provided there is no dehydration or malnutrition, our skin does not wrinkle easily. As a young man said to me in New York, 'Black don't crack.'

Essentially, fibroblasts in brown skin types are larger, but there is a flip side to this. It is the reason brown skin scars more easily and why laser surgery gives better results with white skin (which is why most plastic surgery books feature results on white-skinned individuals). The darker the skin shade, the larger the fibroblast and propensity for scarring. As we noted earlier, melanocytes are present in the basal layer of the epidermis, but they are also located in the bulb of hair follicles. This is why locations with denser hair growth, like armpits and groin, are more prone to pigmentation or darker discolouration of skin.

When the injury is deeper and involves the dermis, fibroblasts from the surrounding areas start producing collagen to fill in the injured area. It is akin to manufacturing cement to fill in a wall that has been breached or damaged.

It used to be thought that keeping a wound dry or allowing it to dry in sunlight helped the wound to heal. In actual fact, the most important way to heal a wound is to rehydrate it and keep it moist. This is all the more important for brown skin where the skin is more likely to form scars. Even for surface scrapes or burns, it is important to keep the wound moist. Even applying petroleum jelly or paraffin will make the wound heal faster and help reduce pigmentation after injury.

When skin is exposed to sun for prolonged periods, the body gets overheated and the blood vessels open so that blood gets closer to the outer surfaces of the body and can therefore cool down. In brown skin type, blood vessels are located deeper in the skin, whereas in blonde or redhead types, blood vessels are closer to the surface. This is why brown skin is less prone to developing red cheeks.

Brown skin is more prone to oiliness as the skin has more hair follicles as well as more oil (sebaceous) glands. The role of these sebaceous glands is not well defined. As they serve to make the skin oily, their primary purpose seems to hydrate the skin. Brown-skinned men are generally hairier and have oilier skin (which leads to their noses appearing shiny, for instance). Male skin is less prone to dehydration. So, while women in general are more conscious of taking care of their skin, it is true that men need less moisturizing than women.

Key points

AVOIDING LOSS OF MOISTURE

- Avoid soap; use soap-free cleansers instead.
- Avoid very hot baths.
- Moisturize skin daily, especially after a bath or shower.
- After swimming in chlorinated pools, shower with normal water and then moisturize.
- Do not exfoliate or scrub skin more than once a week if you have dry skin.

20

Age v. Lifestyle

I smoke a little when I am with friends, say after we have had a few drinks at a nightclub. I am worried my skin is looking old and lifeless. My mother's photos of when she was my age look so much better. Is there anything I can do to look younger?

...

I will go over key concepts of skin ageing in Asian and brown skin types.

It is important to distinguish between intrinsic or 'normal' ageing of skin and 'weather-beaten' photo-ageing, or ageing due to the sun's rays. At high altitudes where the air is purer and pollution less, more UV rays reach the ground. Hence we notice the weather-beaten and wrinkled appearance of people in the Himalayan belt and amongst the Sherpas (of course smoking too hastens wrinkling, as we will discuss). UV radiation studies on Asian skin have shown that sun exposure of more than five hours per day, as in labourers, is associated with nearly five times the risk of wrinkling when compared to those with only a couple of hours' exposure. So it is wise to avoid excessive sun exposure, especially peak sun hours (noon to 3 p.m.). It is advisable to wear a hat or cap if you need to be out in the sun. Using sunscreen is essential if you are out in the sun during peak hours.

As brown skin has more pigmentation due to melanocyte activity, the effects of photo-ageing are different from that of white skin. The chief sign of ageing in brown skin is changes in the pigmentation of skin, rather than wrinkling; the opposite of what happens in white skin.

Studies have shown that smokers are more than twice (studies show two to five times) as likely to develop wrinkles when compared to non-smokers. During a recent visit to Bangalore, I was meeting some friends at a bar and was astounded by how many young women were smoking heavily indoors, while seemingly conscious about their clothing and appearance. Smoking alone does more damage to your skin than you can repair with cosmetics.

As brown skin ages, the capacity to absorb Vitamin D is further reduced. As it is, brown skin has a lower ability to produce Vitamin D and hence supplementation is essential.

So if you want skin to look younger, the old advice still stands: avoid exposure to the sun during peak hours, avoid smoking and moisturize skin to maintain epidermal health. Retinoic acid, which is really an irritant form of Vitamin A, helps make collagen and elastin (photo-ageing related to UV damage is known to reduce elastin production). Therefore, it helps reduce sun damage, especially if used at night as before sun exposure. But consult your cosmetic dermatologist to see if this is indicated for you. Also, don't use a retinoid and then expose yourself to the sun straightaway. We earlier discussed the benefits of the Vitamin B niacin. While AHA (alpha hydroxy-acids) are similarly promoted, in scientific studies, they have not shown the good effects of retinoic acids in the context of photo-ageing. However, Omega-3 in fish oils does show reduction in the effects of photo-ageing, and the antioxidant effect of Vitamin C also has shown benefits. Other foods that we know are beneficial are broccoli, tropical ginger and dark grapes. The younger your skin looks, the fitter you are internally, so your skin basically reflects good health and lifestyle.

One of the problems in brown skin is the increase in pigmentation or spots as we get older. Topical options to deal with this include retinoid creams, niacin-containing creams or gels, lactic acid gels, azelaic acid creams and, depending on the cause, sometimes topical steroid creams. The interesting thing about retinoids is that while they themselves can cause photosensitivity, pretreatment of skin reduces the effects of skin ageing. In other words, using a retinoid at night may help reduce damage, which is why they are widely used by dermatologists in India for skin pigmentation. It is best you see a skin doctor to assess the cause of your pigmentation and plan specific treatments, if your cosmetics have not helped. Some cosmetics may contain retinoids such as retinyl palmitate and help reduce pigmentation. Retinyl palmitate gets converted to retinoic acid when it is applied topically onto skin.

From the over-the-counter cosmetics point of view, potent Vitamin C serums are perhaps the most effective in removing specific spots, especially if you target the spots early. In my research lab, I have developed some high-concentration serums designed to help remove spots. The earlier you treat pigmentation the better, otherwise cosmetic treatment options are limited and you will need to consult a doctor.

In the context of ageing, telomere length has fascinated both researchers and media alike. There seems to finally be a way of assessing ageing by looking at our DNA. But does this apply to skin ageing as well?

Essentially, a chromosome has strands of DNA, and at each end there is a telomere. Each time the cell divides, the genetic information is copied. However, during this copying process, the telomere gets shorter because the cell does not need to preserve this tip. The telomere itself stores no genetic information, but rather acts as a divider or a bookend between 'books' storing genetic coding. Therefore, as the cells divide, the telomere becomes shorter and shorter, while the rest of the length of the DNA strand storing genetic information is preserved. It's like sharpening a pencil – after a certain point, the graphite inside the pencil is too short to sharpen. This was discovered by a scientist and named (after him) as the Hayflick Limit. Cancer cells, for example, have an enzyme called telomerase and therefore can keep reproducing longer than normal cells. Hence research has focused on increasing telomere length and therefore delaying the effects of ageing in normal cells. A large study done in over 2,500 nurses showed the following:

- Dietary fibre intake, especially cereal, like oats, increased telomere length.
- Although fat intake per se made no difference to telomere length, surprisingly, linoleic acid intake reduced telomere length (linoleic acid is found in safflower oil and soybean oil).
- Waist circumference is inversely proportional to telomere length, i.e., the fatter your waist, the shorter your telomeres become.
- Interestingly, smoking and exercise (while having major bad and good effects on cardiovascular health) and hormone replacement therapy did not alter telomere length.
- Sunflower seeds are good. Green tea is good, as is turmeric (the former contains catechins and the latter curcumin, both of which help reduce stress responses that worsen ageing).
- This led researchers to look at whether the telomere length had any association with skin ageing (as opposed to general ageing). Studies on skin ageing showed interesting aspects.

- Epidermis has shorter telomeres when compared to dermis, which may indicate the shorter lifespan of epidermal cells or that they have no 'live' cells.
- Telomere length in the epidermis and in the dermis proportionally reduced with age.
- Interestingly, sun exposure, which caused visible effects of skin ageing, did not lead to shortening of telomeres, suggesting that telomere length may not have the same significance for skin cells, as it does for cells in other bodily tissues.

Key points

- There is a difference between intrinsic ageing and photo-ageing; while brown skin has less intrinsic ageing, photo-ageing due to sun exposure is more predominant.

- Pigmentation due to photo-ageing is more of a concern in brown skin than wrinkles.

- Wrinkling can occur prematurely in smokers and those exposed to sun for long hours without protective clothing or sunscreens.

- In cosmetics, Vitamin C serums and citrus fruits help to remove pigmentation.

- In medical treatments, retinoids and niacin have been shown to reduce the effects of photo-ageing and pigmentation; cosmetics containing retinoids may help.

- Telomere length of DNA is shortened as the cells age and divide.

- Cereals like oats positively affect telomere length; increased girth negatively impacts telomere length.

- Telomere length has not shown a specific link to skin ageing (as opposed to ageing of other bodily cells).

- As brown skin ages, it reduces its capacity to produce Vitamin D; fish oil has very high Vitamin D content.

21

Lasers v. Safety

You've mentioned that lasers might be useful for pigmentation, but also that laser surgery is not good for brown skin. Is this true? Also, how exactly does laser surgery work? How effective is laser hair removal? ...

Physics has always fascinated me, so I'd love to tackle this question, explain what lasers are and talk about how they are useful in treating skin conditions.

It works like this: all electrons in an atom carry different energy levels or charges. Electrons on the outside carry more energy than those on the inside, closer to the nucleus. When an electron from a higher-energy zone moves to a lower-energy one, a photon (a particle of light as the name indicates) is generated. Light emitted by the movement of charged particles in this way is called radiation.

But to understand lasers, one must look at stimulated emission. Let's think of an ordinary light bulb and the light emitted by the tungsten filament. Electrons in the filament move at random from high-energy to lower-energy locations. In a stimulated emission, on the other hand, this movement of electrons is brought about by a photon containing exactly corresponding energy levels.

The acronym 'Laser', as many of us know, stands for Light Amplification by Stimulated Emission of Radiation. Lasers essentially involve light energy stimulated as discussed here. Light energy in the electromagnetic spectrum involves ultraviolet light, visible light and infrared light frequencies. As the frequency is increased beyond the visible and laser spectrum, we enter microwave followed by radio frequencies.

A laser device needs three components:

1. Energy source: This can be a gas (like carbon dioxide or argon, which is where terms like carbon dioxide lasers come from) or a solid (like ruby or Nd:YAG, which stands for the crystal neodymium-doped yttrium aluminium garnet);

2. Resonant cavity: This acts like a mirrored wall and reflects photons back into the medium, thereby increasing energy levels;

3. Device used to 'excite' the atom: This can be a continuous light or a pulsed light, or a quasi-continuous flash lamp or shutter (Q-switched laser).

So if you read that a Q-switched carbon dioxide laser was used, you know that carbon dioxide was the energy source and the device was a photography-like shutter device. In a continuous Nd:YAG laser, the energy source will be crystal and the device a quasi-continuous flash lamp.

Now that we've understood lasers, let's see how they actually work on human skin, and brown skin in particular. First of all, lasers that are reflected or that pass through the tissue have no benefit in treatment. To be useful, the laser light needs to be absorbed by the atom or molecule. These are called chromophores. In our body, a well-known biological chromophore is melanin (which gives us our brown colour) and haemoglobin (which gives blood its red colour). Of course, there may be artificial chromophores on skin, like tattoo ink. Essentially, laser treatment consists of selecting the most appropriate medium and device to treat a particular chromophore, and a cooling device to reduce thermal injury afterwards.

When considering lasers to remove pigmentation, we need to first assess whether the pigment is inherent/endogenous or external/artificial, like tattoo ink. The goal is to remove the desired pigment while preserving skin health. However, melanin in the epidermis, i.e., right at the surface, is an unwanted site for absorption of light. This is why darkly pigmented skin is at high risk for epidermal injury during any laser treatment using visible or near-infrared wavelengths less than 1,200 nm.

For individual flat spots that spread like a blot, carbon dioxide laser (10,600 nm) can be used; for very small pigmented particles, like those causing dark circles under the eyes, Q-switched lasers (694 nm) might help.

We now see more multicoloured tattoos rather than the traditional green or henna-ink ones. To remove a tattoo, we essentially select a wavelength that is preferentially absorbed by the coloured pigment. So for blue colour, for instance, ruby laser (694 nm) is used. Similarly, for green colour, alexandrite laser (755 nm), and for red, frequency-doubled Nd:YAG (532 nm) laser are the usual choices.

Black is the easiest to remove as it absorbs all wavelengths and so all the lasers listed here can be used. However, in brown skin, there is a risk of skin developing a white patch afterwards as it may remove melanin as well.

The commonest tattoo removal requests I get are from young women who have tattooed the name of their previous boyfriend on their skin. For some, work is an issue, because many employers do not employ people with visible tattoos at gaming tables (the Sky City Casino in Auckland is an example). Also, however brilliant the tattoo artwork, they do not look good (in my opinion) when the skin ages and becomes less taut. All things considered, temporary (removable) tattoos are the best. Do remember, tattoo removal results are never perfect on brown skin (or on skin in general).

All laser surgeries carry a risk of complications due to the burn inflicted. Because the risk of scarring and post-inflammatory pigment is greater in brown skin, laser must be a last resort for treating pigmentation, not the first line of treatment.

When lasers are used for resurfacing, i.e., to make skin smoother, it is important to remember that a carbon dioxide laser (10,600 nm, i.e., infrared) vaporizes water and causes deeper tissue destruction up to 100 µm. It tightens collagen and is useful for improvement of severe sun damage, especially in white skin. In brown skin, it carries a higher risk of complications, like pigmentation occurring after the treatment. However, the Erbium:YAG laser (2,940 nm) is absorbed by water more than the carbon dioxide laser and penetrates only 3 µm, causing more epidermal ablation but less collagen tightening. As most brown skin patients do not need collagen tightening, the Nd:YAG lasers are more commonly used in India for laser treatment. Longer-pulsed Nd:YAG lasers are also the first choice for hair removal in brown skin.

Newer fractional lasers may be an option for brown skin. Fractional lasers are less invasive devices that deliver a laser beam divided into thousands of tiny treatment zones and target a fraction of the skin at a time. It is almost as if you were altering a TV image pixel by pixel. This treatment has bridged the gap between the ablative (which works mainly on the epidermis) and non-ablative (which works solely on dermal collagen) laser techniques used to treat sun-damaged and ageing skin. Fractional treatment works at both the epidermal and dermal layers of the skin. These laser machines are now available for many different types of lasers: from Erbium:YAG lasers for superficial treatments and carbon dioxide lasers for deeper treatments.

The risks of laser surgery in all brown skin types are scar formation, abnormal pigmentation after laser treatment (white or dark) and, rarely, increase in hair growth.

Careful patient selection is important. I used fractional laser on my sister-in-law to treat pigmentation and she developed post-inflammatory hyperpigmentation, which took many months to settle. It is important that the follow-up is quite close and detailed, something I found difficult with her because she doesn't live close by. No one is immune to complications, so it is important to know how to manage them. It is important that you discuss this with your surgeon or dermatologist before the treatment.

Given that hair removal is one of the commonest uses of laser treatment, let's look at laser hair removal for a moment. Basically, humans have for long tried to remove hair, possibly reflecting our origins as a 'naked ape'. We are all familiar with methods of hair removal like threading, waxing, shaving and plucking. These were all temporary methods. Then electrolysis was developed as a technique of permanent hair removal. However, not only is this tedious and time-consuming, but in darker skin it also carries a serious risk of developing increased dark pigmentation and scarring, especially in those with curly hair.

As laser therapy evolved, it was reserved for Fitzpatrick skin types 1 to 3, i.e., white skin. The risks in brown skin seemed too high. Adapting lasers for brown skin involved using longer wavelengths, longer pulse durations and better cooling devices.

I have described how laser treatment to remove pigment relies on causing tissue damage by 'selective photothermolysis', which means selecting the correct light and temperature source to destroy tissue that needs removing. The idea is to selectively target the chromophore, thereby removing the pigment while protecting normal tissue. However, in the case of hair removal, the fundamental concept of not harming adjacent tissue is modified. The chromophore that is the target in laser hair removal is the hair shaft and bulb, both of which are melanin-rich in brown skin. To be effective at removing hair, the thermal injury needs to go beyond the hair shaft and bulb, and into the hair follicle and stem cells. These stem cells are crucial for hair development and growth. In order to permanently inhibit hair growth, lasers must thermally destroy not only the entire hair follicle but also these cells. Therein lies the fundamental risk of complications with laser hair removal: the fact that there will be some collateral tissue damage for hair removal to be effective.

The absorption spectrum of melanin is in the range of 250–1,200 nm. As we increase the wavelength, there is greater depth of penetration and also less interference with the dark pigment in the epidermis. This is why longer wavelengths work better for brown skin. Also, using longer pulse durations allows for the epidermis to cool and thus reduces the risk of increased pigmentation due to epidermal melanin making a nuisance of itself. In general, if we can keep the epidermal temperature to under 45°C, there is low risk of complication. This is why cooling devices – either a cold plate or spray – are used. In dark skin, one must also be careful of not making the skin too cold, because if the skin becomes effectively frostbitten, it leads to problems with increased pigmentation after the procedure. The Nd:YAG wavelength is inherently safer to treat darker skin types and most Nd:YAG lasers come with their own cooling devices.

There are certain people who should not go for laser hair removal. Those on gold treatment (for rheumatoid arthritis) or St John's wort (a natural anti-depressant), for example. Any such treatment needs to be stopped for at least three months prior to laser hair removal. People on retinoids such as roaccutane or accutane (used for acne) or those with a history of keloid scarring should not opt for laser hair removal.

One of the interesting things about dark skin is that, notwithstanding the increased risk of scarring and pigmentation, laser hair removal actually works better on dark skin than white skin. This is because, as we discussed, melanin acts as a chromatophore. Laser hair removal in blonde hair is often unsuccessful due to lack of melanin. The amount of eumelanin (the darker variant of melanin found in brown and black skin) correlates with the success of laser hair removal.

Intense pulsed light (IPL) is also now used to remove hair. Bizarrely enough, in brown-skinned individuals of Fitzpatrick skin types 4 to 6, IPL may actually increase hair growth. This increase occurs in areas adjacent to where the hair is being removed, and people with hormonal problems like polycystic ovaries syndrome have a higher risk. Therefore, IPL lasers are best avoided in brown skin for hair removal as they may end up causing the opposite effect.

Key points

- Laser treatments are used to remove pigment or hair, and to resurface skin.

- Laser light needs to be absorbed by chromophores; in the body, chromophores are melanin, haemoglobin and tattoo ink.

- To remove a tattoo, we essentially select a wavelength that is preferentially absorbed by the coloured pigment.

- Risks of lasers in brown skin are scar formation, abnormal pigmentation after laser treatment (white or dark) and, rarely, increase in hair growth.

- Tattoo removal results are never perfect.

- Laser hair removal works better in dark skin; IPL can cause increased hair growth.

- When using laser hair removal, longer wavelengths and pulse intervals help reduce complications.

- People on retinoids or those with a history of keloid scars should not undergo laser hair removal.

22

Stretch Marks v. Brown Skin

*I am really worried about stretch marks. I never used to
have them but now I am getting them on my stomach and
thighs. What causes them and is there any solution? ...*

For Latin buffs, 'stretch marks' have a medical term, *striae
distensae*, which simply means lines formed due to distension
or stretch. They can be either white or reddish (*striae albae*
or *striae rubrae*). When caused by pregnancy, they are called
striae gravidarum. In fact, most stretch marks start as the
reddish or purple variant, which then become scar-like and
turn white. The root of the problem is really dermal scarring.

While most stretch marks occur in adolescents and
pregnant women, they can also be caused by medications like
steroids (leading to hypotheses regarding the cause of stretch
marks: inadequate development of elastin and collagen),
mechanical stretch causing fracturing of the dermis and
hormonal imbalance.

Brown and black skins are more likely to develop stretch
marks, as are smokers and those with a high body mass index
(BMI) (those who are overweight or obese as children). Yes,
stretch marks do run in families and among twins, suggesting
a genetic predisposition. Interestingly, young women who

become pregnant are more likely to get stretch marks when compared to women who conceive after age twenty-five. In older women, those with prolapsed uteruses are more likely to get stretch marks showing a fundamental problem with elastin and collagen fibres (under the microscope, collagen fibres are structurally altered; elastin fibres reduced and reorganized; elastin fibres are found in connective tissues like muscles and arteries and help these snap back to normal like a rubber band after stretching).

What can one do about stretch marks? I am presenting some evidence-based advice (see Figure 8 below) about many things that have been tried to reduce or prevent stretch marks:

- Exercise: This has shown no benefit in clinical trials with respect to stretch marks.
- Cocoa butter and olive oil: These have shown no benefit scientifically. Studies involved massaging cocoa butter and olive oil, and in both trials there were no differences between those treated and the untreated control group.
- Tretinoin: This is a retinoid. Remember, we discussed retinoids earlier as they are helpful in severe acne

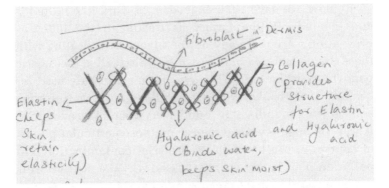

Figure 8: Illustration of collagen, elastin and hyaluronic acid

and also reduce pigmentation. Topically applied, tretinoin creams have shown a reduction in stretch marks. Under the microscope, there was no difference in elastin and, therefore, these creams seem to work by improving collagen production.

- Hyaluronic acid: This naturally occurring compound is also used in beauty treatments. Essentially, it binds water, keeping skin tissues moist. Hyaluronic acid has also shown some benefit, mostly in women who were not overweight.

- Almond oil: In a clinical study, almond oil, when combined with a massage, halved the incidence of stretch marks in pregnant women. Many people have told me that wheatgerm oil is even more effective, but this has not been formally studied.

- Sand abrasion and TCA (trichloroacetic acid): Essentially, this is dermabrasion and a chemical peel using TCA. Not effective in dark or brown skin where it increases pigmentation. (We have already discussed the risks of chemical peels in brown skin, haven't we?) Peels and lasers are, therefore, better avoided in brown skin.

By now, we have a few that seem to work like retinoids and almond oil (the former as treatment; the latter as prevention). Are there any newer advances in dealing with these stretch marks? *Centella asiatica*, also called the Asiatic pennywort or the Indian pennywort, is commonly used for cooking in Sri Lanka, where it is called *gotu kola* (meaning conical leaf). In India, it is found everywhere. I've even seen it grow on open sewage ditches, and those particular plants, of course, would be prone to bacterial contamination and pollution. This is probably the reason why the pennywort is not being used to make creams in India.

However, when used alone in a cream or combined with hyaluronic acid, it has shown some benefit in reducing stretch marks in all skin types. A cream called Trofolastin is marketed, which contains *Centella asiatica*. The authors of a study also claimed a 22 per cent reduction in stretch marks when Trofolastin was used to prevent stretch marks during pregnancy. There appears to be some bias in the study and caution needs to be exercised in interpreting the results, but, overall, this plant has shown some benefit.

Radio-frequency (RF) devices, especially in combination with platelet-rich plasma, also has some benefit, but caution must be exercised in brown skin. Since this is not a medical book, I won't detail this modality.

Key points

- Stretch marks can be white or red in colour.
- They occur more commonly in adolescents or pregnant women; young pregnancies seem to have a higher incidence.
- Almond oil, especially when massaged into skin, has been shown to reduce stretch marks in pregnancy.
- Tretinoin, a retinoid, when used as a cream, has shown improvement in stretch marks.
- *Centella asiatica* has shown promise, and creams containing the plant (either alone or in combination with hyaluronic acid) have shown some benefit.

23

Warts v. Infections

My husband is developing these brown and black warts on his face. He is in his forties and they seem to be getting worse. Are these viral? We Indian people seem to be prone to these warts. ...

It is more than likely that the warty growths you are referring to are not 'true warts'. True warts are medically what we call verruca – a viral infection caused by the human papilloma virus (HPV). While these are contagious and spread, they are usually white in colour and if you shave these warts right down, you will see spots of blood. These specks of blood are actually blood vessels that are nourishing the growth. While various remedies, like freezing and duct-taping have been tried, usually the viral warts go away naturally after approximately four years. It is unlikely that what you are describing is viral, because these are usually localized in an area, even if they can spread. It is more likely that the brown to black lesions you are describing are one of the two I am detailing in the following pages: seborrhoeic keratoses (see Figure 9) and dermatosis papularis nigra lesions (see Figure 10), the most common types in brown skin. Both generally appear after age forty; people develop more lesions as they

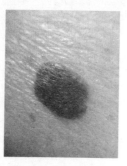

Figure 9: Seborrhoeic
keratoses, the
commonest warty
growths we see on
skin as we age

Figure 10: Dermatosis
papularis nigra
lesions on
the face

get older. If you shave them right down, you will see they are situated atop skin rather like barnacles – the crustaceans that attach themselves onto rocks or ships.

Seborrhoeic keratoses are large warty growths that are brown to black in colour and are more common on the trunk of the body. Their surface is rough and flaky. They are a cosmetic nuisance, and while they can be scraped or shaved and electro-dessicated (pulverizing tissue using radio frequency or a cautery), the idea is to keep the treatment superficial to avoid scarring in brown skin. Dermatosis papularis nigra lesions, on the other hand, are like small seborrhoeic keratoses, but numerous and found commonly on the face. Again, they are harmless, commonly referred to as warts, but are neither viral nor dangerous. For these lesions too the treatment is freezing (cryotherapy), scraping (curettage) or electro-dessication, taking care not to penetrate into the dermis. I personally avoid freezing in brown skin as it can cause either increased or decreased pigmentation (whitish or dark marks). I usually recommend shaving and electro-dessication – and the treatment ought not to leave any marks or long-term scarring. Some people also use Nd:YAG lasers, but I find shaving is much simpler and less risky.

Rarely do we see a warty growth that has a reddish inflamed area around the lesion, which in turn keeps growing or changing. As a skin cancer specialist, I recognize these as squamous cell cancers, sometimes found in brown skin. Interestingly, a cousin of mine was visiting from New Delhi and had a lesion on his thigh. He had consulted a dermatologist back home and was told it was a wart and could be left alone. I guess because skin cancer is so common in New Zealand, it was easier for me to diagnose this. I removed this lesion and sure enough the biopsy confirmed a squamous cell cancer. If a lesion is changing or growing, or has signs of inflammation – reddish or pinkish areas around the warty growth – don't assume it is harmless. It is better to be biopsied (sample taken for testing under the microscope) to make a definite diagnosis. Squamous cell cancers can spread to lymph nodes if not treated, and can be dangerous.

Key points

- All warty growths are not viral; viral warts are usually whitish and contagious.

- In brown skin, warty growths are common and are usually harmless and can be removed by scraping, shaving surgically or electro-dessication.

- If a warty growth appears inflamed at the edges and is growing, seek medical help to make sure it is not a skin cancer.

24

Feet v. Odour

Help! I've got stinky feet and it is losing me girlfriends!
Have you got any solutions or suggestions?   ...

When my editor canvassed opinions as to what people would like covered in this book, this was a topic that was raised. W.H. Auden once said*: *A man has his distinctive personal scent which his wife, his children and his dog can recognize. A crowd has a generalized stink. The public is odourless.*

One of the things we doctors do is lend conditions gravitas – the medical term for 'smelly feet' is *bromodosis*. What's wrong with just saying stinky feet? Maybe for a diagnosis like that we couldn't charge a fee. Just a thought.

Foot odour is very common. I do skin checks all day and, as people have to take off their shoes and socks, it is something I encounter very often. This is not a specific issue for brown skin, so I did not tackle it here.

For a start, foot odour is more common if you are a teenager, pregnant, under emotional stress and stand all day at work. Of course people who have excessively sweaty feet are more

* Nina Eliasoph. *Avoiding Politics: How Americans Produce Apathy in Everyday Life*, Cambridge, UK: Cambridge University Press, 1998, p. 281.

prone to having smelly feet; sweaty feet are also more prone to fungal diseases like athlete's foot and this worsens the odour. There are more sweat glands in our feet than anywhere else in our body. In teenagers and pregnant women this is aggravated, mainly for hormonal reasons.

The reason sweaty feet cause foot odour is because we sweat into our shoes all day and when we take them off the shoes are damp. Bacteria love these moist, dark and warm (from body heat) conditions. There is a particular bacterium that loves to colonize sweat as it comes out of the pores. These bacteria – with important-sounding names like *Micrococcus sedentarius* – produce organic acids and sulphur compounds that smell like rotten eggs. Even after we remove our shoes, the bacteria continue to multiply. Shoes take more than a day to dry out. Therefore, if you put on the same pair of shoes the next day, even if you have showered, you have not allowed enough time for the shoes to dry out. One simple remedy is to alternate your shoes, i.e., never wear the same pair on consecutive days.

Here are a few remedies that we know are beneficial and reduce foot odour. Since the key is to avoid sweat and reduce bacterial colony contamination, dabbing surgical spirit on the feet, especially between the toes, helps dry out these surfaces. Using an underarm deodorant works just as well. You can use a stick, roll-on or a spray. Just use on feet and allow to dry before you put on your socks. Leather or canvas footwear is better than plastic footwear, as the latter sweat more. Going barefoot at home helps, as does wearing open sandals in summer.

The above reduce sweating; to reduce bacterial contamination, I have found chlorhexidine, which we use as a surgical scrub called hibitane or hibiscrub, very useful. This works because chlorhexidine gluconate is an antiseptic effective against a wide range of bacteria, yeasts, some fungi and viruses. In a National Health Service (NHS) review of smelly feet in the UK, Lorraine Jones, a chiropodist, was even more enthusiastic: 'If you already have foot odour, the good news is that there's a simple, quick solution.' Just wash your feet twice a day in chlorhexidine; this generally fixes the problem within a week.

Key points

- Stinky feet are more common in teenagers and pregnant women.

- It is the combination of sweat and bacterial contamination that causes foot odour.

- Avoiding wearing the same shoe two days in a row helps reduce foot odour; leather or canvas is preferable to plastic or synthetics.

- Underarm deodorant works to reduce foot sweating and odour; rubbing surgical spirit between toes also helps.

- Chlorhexidine gluconate (commonly found in surgical scrubs like hibiscrub) is the most effective remedy. Washing feet twice a day in chlorhexidine generally fixes the problem within a week.

References

1. A.A. Qureshi, P.L. Dominguez, H.K. Choi, J. Han and G. Curhan, 'Alcohol Intake and Risk of Incident Psoriasis in US Women: A Prospective Study', *Arch. Dermatol.*, vol. 146, no. 12, 2010, pp. 1364–69.

2. Aedín Cassidy, Immaculata De Vivo, Yan Liu, Jiali Han, Jennifer Prescott, David J. Hunter and Eric B. Rimm, 'Associations between Diet, Lifestyle Factors and Telomere Length in Women', *American Journal of Clinical Nutrition*, vol. 91, no. 5, 2010, pp. 1273–80.

3. A. De Groot, I.R. White, M.A. Flyvholm, G. Lensen and P.J. Coenraads, 'Formaldehyde-releasers in Cosmetics: Relationship to Formaldehyde Contact Allergy', *Contact Dermatitis*, vol. 62, no. 1, 2010, pp. 18–31.

4. Carmen Cabrera, Reyes Artacho and Rafael Giménez, 'Beneficial Effects of Green Tea – A Review', *Journal of the American College of Nutrition*, vol. 25, no. 2, 2006, pp. 79–99.

5. C.P. Sambucco, P.D. Forbes, R.E. Davies and F. Urbach, 'Protective Value of Skin Tanning Induced by Ultraviolet Radiation Plus a Sunscreen Containing Bergamot Oil', *Journal of the Society of Cosmetic Chemists*, vol. 38, 1987, pp. 11–19.

6. Craig A. Elmets and Alexandra Zhang, 'Common Photosensitizing Medications and Chemicals', *SCF Guide to Sunscreens,* Skin Cancer Foundation Inc., 2007, http://www.skincancer.org/prevention/sun-protection/sunscreen/the-skin-cancer-foundations-guide-to-sunscreens, accessed 1 May 2014.

7. C. Young, 'Niacinamide: Reversibility of Reduction of Facial Hyperpigmented Spots', *Journal of the American Academy of Dermatology*, vol. 52, no. 3, ISSN 0190-9622.

8. D.L. Bissett, K. Miyamoto, P. Sun, J. Li and C.A. Berge, 'Topical Niacinamide Reduces Yellowing, Wrinking, Red Blotchiness and Hyperpigmented Spots in Ageing Facial Skin', *International Journal of Cosmetic Science*, vol. 26, no. 5, 2004, ISSN 0142-5463.

9. D.L. Bissett, J.E. Oblong and C.A. Berge, 'Niacinamide: A B Vitamin that Improves Ageing Facial Skin Appearance', *Dermatology Surgery*, vol. 31, no. 7, 2005, ISSN 1076-0512.

10. D. Deidre, R.N. Wipke-Tevis and Donna A. Williams, 'Effect of Oral Hydration on Skin Microcirculation in Healthy Young and Midlife and Older Adults', *Wound Repair and Regeneration*, vol. 15, no. 2, 2007, pp. 174–85.

11. D.P. Kadunce, R. Burr, R. Gress, R. Kanner, J.L. Lyon and J.J. Zone, 'Cigarette Smoking: Risk Factor for Premature Facial Wrinkling', *Annals of Internal Medicine*, vol. 114, 1991, pp. 840–44.

12. E. Battle, 'Laser Hair Removal for Darker Skin Types', in *Skin of Colour*, New York: Springer.

13. E.H. Spencer, H.R. Ferdowsian and N.D. Barnard, 'Diet and Acne: A Review of the Evidence', *International Journal of Dermatology*, vol. 48, no. 4, 2009, pp. 339–47.

14. 'Electromagnetic spectrum', New World Encyclopedia, http://www.newworldencyclopedia.org/entry/Electromagnetic_spectrum?oldid=679396, accessed 17 June 2011.

15. Emily Tierney and David Goldberg, 'Laser Hair Removal Pearls: Review Article', *Journal of Cosmetic and Laser Therapy*, vol. 10, no. 1, 2008, pp. 17–23.

16. Elma D. Baron, Eugene B. Kirkland and Diana Santo Domingo, 'Advances in Photoprotection', *Dermatology Nursing*, vol. 20, no. 4, 2008, pp. 265–73.

17. Esther Boelsma, Henk F.J. Hendriks and Len Roza, 'Nutritional Skin Care: Health Effects of Micronutrients and Fatty Acids', *The American Journal of Clinical Nutrition*, vol. 73, no. 5, 2001, pp. 853–64.

18. Fernanda Magagnin Freitag and Tania Ferreira Cestari, 'What Causes Dark Circles Under the Eyes?' *Journal of Cosmetic Dermatology*, vol. 6, no. 3, 2007, pp. 211–15.

19. Françoise Arnold, Michel Mercier and My Trinh Luu, 'Metabolism

of Vitamin D in Skin: Benefits for Skin Care Applications', *Journal of Cosmetics & Toiletries*, vol. 124, no. 10, pp. 40–46.

20. Frederick Skiff, 'Einstein and the Laser', Seminar notes, LR1 Van Allen Hall University of Iowa, October 2005.

21. H.A. Bischoff-Ferrari, W.C. Willett, J.B. Wong, E. Giovannucci, T. Dietrich and B. Dawson-Hughes, 'Fracture Prevention with Vitamin D Supplementation: A Meta-analysis of Randomized Controlled Trials', *Journal of the American Medical Association*, vol. 293, 2005, pp. 2257–64.

22. H.L. Dhar, 'Approach to Anti-ageing', *Bombay Hospital Journal*, vol. 51, no. 1, 2009.

23. How To Stop Smelly Feet – Live Well – NHS Choices, http://www.nhs.uk/Livewell/foothealth/Pages/smellyfeet.aspx, accessed 1 June 2007.

24. Jacobo Wortsman, Lois Y. Matsuoka, Tai C. Chen, Zhiren Lu and Michael F. Holick, 'Decreased Bioavailability of Vitamin D in Obesity', *The American Journal of Clinical Nutrition*, vol. 72, no. 3, 2000, pp. 690–3.

25. Jeff Evans, 'Contact Dermatitis in Auto Mechanic? Think Isothiazolinones', *Family Practice News*, 2005.

26. J.H. Chung, S.H. Lee, C.S. Youn, Byung Joo Park, Kyu Han Kim, Kyung Chan Park, Kwang Hyun Cho and Hee Chul Eun, 'Cutaneous Photodamage in Koreans: Influence of Sex, Sun-exposure, Smoking and Skin Color', *Arch. Dermatol.*, vol. 137, no. 8, 2001, pp. 1043–51.

27. Julia K. Padgett, 'Cutaneous Lasers', *Dermpath MD*, 30 January 2004, www.dermpathmd.com/cases/dermatopathology.../Cutaneous%20Lasers.pdf, accessed 18 June 2011.

28. J.Y. Jung, M.Y. Yoon, S.U. Min, J.S. Hong, Y.S. Choi and D.H. Suh, 'The Influence of Dietary Patterns on Acne Vulgaris in Koreans', *European Journal of Dermatology*, vol. 20, no. 6, 2010, pp. 768–72.

29. Knut Brockow, Volker Steinkraus, Franz Rinninger, Dietrich-Abeck and Johannes Ring, 'Acanthosis Nigricans: A Marker for Hyperinsulinemia', *Pediatric Dermatology*, vol. 12, no. 4, 1995, pp. 323–26.

30. Kotaro Yoshimura, Kiyonori Harii, Takao Aoyama and Tatsuji Iga, 'Experience with a Strong Bleaching Treatment for Skin

Hyperpigmentation in Orientals', *Plastic & Reconstructive Surgery*, vol. 105, no. 3, 2000, pp. 1097–1108.

31. L. Baumann, *The Skin Type Solution*, New York: Bantam Books.

32. Lesley E. Rhodes, Sheryl O'Farrell, Malcolm J. Jackson and Peter S. Friedmann, 'Dietary Fish-oil Supplementation in Humans Reduces UVB-Erythemal Sensitivity But Increases Epidermal Lipid Peroxidation', *Journal of Investigative Dermatology*, vol. 103, no. 2, 1994, pp. 151–54.

33. M.A. Gupta, N.J. Schork, A.K. Gupta and C.N. Ellis, 'Alcohol Intake and Treatment Responsiveness of Psoriasis: A Prospective Study', *Journal of the American Academy of Dermatology*, vol. 28, no. 5, pt 1, 1993, pp. 730–2.

34. Mark Lees, *The Skin Care Answer Book*, New York: Milady Cengage Learning, 2011.

35. Michael Wooldridge, Linus Pauling lectures on Vitamin C and Heart Disease, Life Sciences Division's Lipoprotein and Atherosclerosis Group Seminar, 1993, MAWooldridge@lbl.gov

36. Miho Sugimotoa, Ritsuo Yamashita and Masato Uedab, 'Telomere Length of the Skin in Association with Chronological Ageing and Photoageing', *Journal of Dermatological Science*, vol. 43, no. 1, 2006, pp. 43–47.

37. M.K.B. Bogh, A.V. Schmedes, P.A. Philipsen, E. Thieden and H.C. Wulf, 'Interdependence between Body Surface Area and Ultraviolet B Dose in Vitamin D Production: A Randomized Controlled Trial', *British Journal of Dermatology*, vol. 164, no. 1. 2011, ISSN 0007-0963.

38. Muneer T., Asif M. and Munawwar S., 'Sustainable Production of Solar Electricity with Particular Reference to the Indian Economy', *Renewable & Sustainable Energy Reviews*, vol. 9, no. 5, 2005, pp. 444–73.

39. Murad Alam, A.C. Bhatia, R.V. Kundu, S.S. Yoo and H.H. Chan, *Cosmetic Dermatology for Skin of Colour*, New York: Mc-Graw Hill, 2009.

40. P.D. Darbre, A. Aljarrah, W.R. Miller, N.G. Coldham, M.J. Sauer and G.S. Pope, 'Concentrations of Parabens in Human Breast Tumours', *Journal of Applied Toxicology*, vol. 24, no. 1, 2004, pp. 5–13.

41. Raj Kubba, A.K. Bajaj, D.M. Thappa, Rajeev Sharma, Maya Vedamurthy, Sandipan Dhar, S. Criton, Rui Fernandez, A.J. Kanwar, Uday Khopkar, Malavika Kohli, V.P. Kuriyipe, Koushik Lahiri, Nina Madnani, Deepak Parikh, Sudhir Pujara, K.K. Rajababu, S. Sacchidanand, V.K. Sharma and Jayakar Thomas, 'Factors Precipitating or Aggravating Acne', *Acne in India: Guidelines for Management – IAA Consensus Document*, vol. 75, no. 7, 2009, pp. 10–12.

42. Richard A. Baxter, 'Anti-ageing Properties of Resveratrol: Review and Report of a Potent New Antioxidant Skin Care Formulation', *Journal of Cosmetic Dermatology*, vol. 7, no. 1, 2008, pp. 2–7.

43. R.P. Heaney, 'Long-latency Deficiency Disease: Insights from Calcium and Vitamin D', *The American Journal of Clinical Nutrition*, vol. 78, 2003, pp. 912–9.

44. R.J. Shephard and P.N. Shek, 'Potential Impact of Physical Activity and Sport on the Immune System: A Brief Review', *British Journal of Sports Medicine*, vol. 4, no. 28, pp. 247–55.

45. R. Lindberg, 'Active Living: On the Road with the 10,000 Steps Program', *Journal of the American Dietetic Association*, vol. 100, 2000, pp. 878–79.

46. R. Nowack, V.K. Singh and J.N. Govil, 'Herbal Treatments for Renal Diseases', *Phytopharmacology and Therapeutic Values*, vol. III, 2008, pp. 317–31.

47. R.R. Anderson and J.A. Parrish, 'The Optics of Human Skin', *Journal of Investigative Dermatology*, vol. 77, 1981, pp. 13–19.

48. S. Al-Himdani, S. Ud-Din, S. Gilmore and A. Bayat, 'Striae Distensae: A Comprehensive Review and Evidence-based Evaluation of Prophylaxis and Treatment', *British Journal of Dermatology*, vol. 170, no. 3, 2014, pp. 527–47.

49. S. Block, F.W. Danby and J. Keri, *American Academy of Dermatology*, 69th Annual Meeting: Abstract 305, presented on 6 February 2011.

50. Shruti Goel, 'Bioprotective Properties of Turmeric: An Investigation of the Antioxidant and Antimicrobial Activities', *Journal of Young Investigators*, vol. 21, no. 6, 2011.

51. Stephen Hsu, 'Green Tea and the Skin', *Journal of the American Academy of Dermatology*, vol. 52, no. 6, 2005, pp. 1049–59.

52. T.B. Fitzpatrick, 'The Validity and Practicality of Sun-reactive Skin Types I through VI', *Arch. Dermatol.*, vol. 124, no. 6, 1988, pp. 869–71.

53. T. Hakozaki, R.E. Boissy, L. Minwalla, J. Zhuang, M. Chhoa, A. Matsubara, K. Miyamoto, A. Greatens, G.G. Hillebrand and D.L. Bissett, 'The Effect of Niacinamide on Reducing Cutaneous Pigmentation and Suppression of Melanosome Transfer', *British Journal of Dermatology*, vol. 147, no. 1, 2002, ISSN 0007-0963.

54. University of Illinois Eye and Ear Infirmary, 'Nutrition, Vitamins, and Eye Vision.' *The Eye Digest*, 2003.

55. W. Montagna and K. Carlisle, 'The Architecture of Black and White Facial Skin', *Journal of the American Academy of Dermatology*, vol. 24, no. 6, 1991, pp. 929–37.

56. World Health Organization, 'The Known Health Effects of UV: What Are the Effects of UV on the Eye?' WHO Report: Ultraviolet Radiation and the INTERSUN Programme, 2008, http://www.who.int/uv/faq/uvhealtfac/en/index3.html, accessed 1 May 2014.

57. Z.D. Draelos, A. Matsubara and K. Smiles, 'The Effect of 2% Niacinamide on Facial Sebum Production', *Journal of Cosmetic and Laser Therapy*, vol. 8, no. 2, 2006.